ENVISION

STUDENT WORKBOOK

Jason Evert, Brian Butler, and Colin & Aimee MacIver

ASCENSION

West Chester, Pennsylvania

Nihil obstat: Robert A. Pesarchick, STD
               Censor librorum
               April 22, 2024

Imprimatur: +Most Rev. Nelson J. Perez, DD
               Archbishop of Philadelphia
               April 26, 2024

Ascension
PO Box 1990
West Chester, PA 19380
1-800-376-0520
ascensionpress.com

Cover design: Stella Ziegler, Faceout Studio
Printed in United States of America

ISBN: 978-1-954882-52-2

Contents

Lesson One: Who Am I?

DISCOVERING MY IDENTITY, PURPOSE, AND DESTINY

OPENING PRAYER

+ In the name of the Father, and of the Son, and of the Holy Spirit. Amen.

In the divine image, Lord, you created him; male and female you created them. Lord, you made us body and soul for relationship. You created us from love and for love without anything to hide from you. God, you made us to be happy with you forever.

Jesus, you taught us to address your Father as you did, and so,
in the Holy Spirit, we pray, *Our Father* ... Amen.

"It is Jesus ... you seek when you dream of happiness; he is waiting for you when nothing else you find satisfies you; he is the beauty to which you are so attracted; it is he who provokes you with that thirst for fullness that will not let you settle for compromise; it is he who urges you to shed the masks of a false life; it is he who reads in your hearts your most genuine choices, the choices that others try to stifle."

—St. John Paul II, World Youth Day, Rome, 2000

THE BIG PICTURE

You are a unique and unrepeatable masterpiece.

Yes, you.

This is just the truth. The same God who made stars, mountains, lions, sharks, trees, and roses made *you*. You are more wonderfully and powerfully made than any other creature. You are created in God's image and likeness—created by love, for love, by a God who loves you wildly. And God wants you to experience joy with him forever.

As you begin this program, you're going through the struggles and problems of ordinary life—school and work, boredom and stress. Maybe you're just trying to make it to the weekend. You want to be free and happy, but sometimes it's hard to know what to choose. How can you believe that you are so greatly loved and destined for such greatness? How can this truth become real for you?

It's not enough to just be told. If this awesome truth of who you are and what you're made for is going to have any impact on your everyday life, you will have to discover it, encounter it, and enter into it. You'll have to ask big questions about who you are, where you're headed, and how to get there. You'll need guidance, courage, and persistence. You'll need a true, total vision of who you really are and how you should live.

That's the exact goal of St. John Paul II's Theology of the Body. Theology of the Body helps us understand who we are, what we are made for, and how to live and love in a broken world. It's about real life and real love and will take real openness on your part.

Are you ready?

STORY STARTER

At age eight, I decided to run away from home so I could drink orange juice whenever I wanted.

In my family, orange juice was a special treat for birthdays and holidays. My four siblings and I could gulp down multiple gallons of juice a day, which got to be pretty expensive, so my mom had stopped buying orange juice as an everyday beverage.

If I ran away, I thought, I could buy my own juice and whatever else made me happy. Maybe I would also get some Cocoa Puffs and Froot Loops to replace Mom's standard menu of Cheerios and bananas. I'd have as much as I wanted, whenever I wanted. I couldn't wait to be my own person and follow my own rules!

My friend Paul agreed to join me. Neither of us had any serious problems at home; we just wanted to be free. We met up one morning after my mom left the house to run errands. With plastic grocery bags in hand, we went through the house to gather up what we thought we would need for our journey and new life. Clothes, of course, but definitely not church clothes. And maybe some medicine, but only the yummy chewable pills, not that nasty syrup.

As we got ready to leave, Paul suggested bringing a few "survival" books to help us figure out which plants we could eat. This was before smart devices and search engines, so we settled on packing my family's set of encyclopedias. Paul and I put several heavy books into plastic bags and headed out the door.

At first, we were too excited to notice how heavy our bags were. We talked about where we would set up camp and how to start a fire with two sticks as we'd seen on shows. But soon, the summer sun reached its full intensity. We started sweating as we dragged the bags along the road. Had they been this heavy when we left the house?

Though neither of us wanted to admit it, we soon realized that we had made a mistake. Maybe running away and living by our own rules wasn't quite as fun and exciting as we'd imagined. Things were pretty good at home. Our attempted adventure ended with Paul going back to his house and me climbing into my bunk bed that night.

Paul and I wanted to be free to make our own choices. We thought that doing whatever we wanted would make us happy. But we had no idea how to use our freedom. We knew we needed something to guide us, but we packed all the wrong things and didn't even make it out of the neighborhood. We thought we had it all figured out, but we were really clueless about what it meant to "be our own person" and how to take care of ourselves.

It would be years before either of us could set out on our own. First, we needed to know who we really were, what real freedom and happiness look like, and how to get there.—*Aimee MacIver*

IF YOU ASK ME ...

- *If I had to leave home tonight and could take only one thing with me, I would take* _____.

- *If I were on my own, one house rule I would not follow is* _____.

- *I think what everyone really wants most is* _____.

- *I think the reason God made us is* _____.

Video 1: Introduction

IF YOU ASK ME ...

- *Who are you? How would you describe yourself without saying your name?* _____

_____

Video 2: To the Core

VIDEO QUESTIONS

1. **True or False:** "Who we are" refers to who likes or dislikes us.

2. **True or False:** You cannot make God love you any more than he does right now.

3. **True or False:** The more you love others, the more you will understand who you are and how much God loves you.

Who are you?

If you walked into a room full of strangers and had to identify yourself without using your name, what would you say? Would you describe your relationships? *"I am Henry's granddaughter." "I am Michelle's brother."* Would you give some details of your personality? *"I am shy." "I am outgoing."* You could explain what you do: *"I am a soccer player." "I am a dancer."* You could share your likes: *"I like pizza." "I like riding horses."*

All these things describe parts of your identity. As you go through life, you will discover more and more about your unique likes, dislikes, needs, desires, and personality traits. But underneath everything else, who are you as a human person? The deepest question is, What is the core of your identity?

You've been trying to figure out your identity since you were really young.

It probably started with learning your name and your age. Then you and your friends began spending hours pretending to be different characters: firefighters, ballerinas, football stars, chefs, veterinarians, teachers, and more. Most kids play games about being grown up. Why? Why don't you see first graders running around the playground saying, "Let's pretend to be first graders"? Even from an early age, why were you motivated to become more than you are now?

It's because your identity is more—much more—than any job or lifestyle. From the moment we are conceived, before we are even born and begin discovering our personalities, our core identity already exists. As **human persons**, we are created in God's image and likeness. This means we are God's sons and daughters. God made us for our own sake—just so he could love us and we could return that love. Love cannot be forced. It must be freely chosen, so God also made us free to choose.

So who are you? No matter what happens to you and no matter what choices you make, your core identity as God's son or daughter will never change. You don't have to earn God's love, and you can never lose it.

> "God, infinitely perfect and blessed in himself, in a plan of sheer goodness freely created man to make him share in his own blessed life. For this reason, at every time and in every place, God draws close to man. He calls man to seek him, to know him, to love him with all his strength."
>
> —Catechism of the Catholic Church, 1

IF YOU ASK ME ...

- *Something that makes human beings different from animals is* _____.

- *A relationship that is important to my identity is* _____.

Freedom and happiness

As human persons, we have deep desires for freedom and happiness. At this point in your life, you probably feel the urge to have more freedom and make more of your own choices. Sometimes you might feel restless or annoyed when parents or teachers tell you what to do, simply because you want to do your own thing, not theirs. This desire is natural and necessary to help you discover who you are and who you want to become.

In fact, your desire for freedom and happiness is part of God's design. God created us with these desires so that we would look for him, find him, and freely choose to love him—which is the source of true happiness.

As we grow up, this process of choosing for ourselves gets more complicated. When you were a kid, free choices were pretty simple: Should you choose chocolate or vanilla ice cream? Happiness also came pretty easily in childhood. Some candy and new toys pretty much did it. You spent all day playing and napping, and your biggest responsibility was washing your hands before dinner. Your friends didn't care about your clothes or popularity. If you wanted to impress them, you jumped on your bed or blew bubbles in your milk. Nobody was seriously concerned with crushes or dating or having boyfriends or girlfriends.

Now your choices have higher stakes: If you speak up in class, will you look stupid? Should you hang out with your friends and risk failing tomorrow's test, or should you miss the fun to study? You are expected to keep up your grades, practice hard, complete your chores, and help out at home. Your group of friends is changing. You may find out you don't have much in common anymore with old friends from elementary school. You may have more interest in relationships beyond friendship. You may feel more concerned with your looks and more confused about how to be accepted. The changes—and the choices that go with them—can be pretty overwhelming. What should you wear? What should you say? Will people like you?

You want freedom to make your own choices, but sometimes you don't know what to choose. You want to find happiness, but sometimes you're not sure where to look. This is exactly when it matters most to know who you are and where you're headed.

IF YOU ASK ME ...

- *A choice I have a hard time making is* _____.

- *One thing I want to start choosing for myself is* _____.

Where are you going?

Imagine that you're hiking to a certain destination in the forest. To get there, you will have to choose between many trails and make many turns. If you try to travel by just randomly choosing directions, you will get lost. You could walk all day and be no closer to your goal—maybe even farther away than when you started. You

can get to your destination only if you follow trail signs or a map.

Life can be like this, too. We don't find freedom and happiness by doing whatever we feel like in the moment. If we want to end up really free and happy, we need directions. Where should we look for examples of what it means to be a free, happy person?

Both in real life and online, the examples can be confusing. Many older teens seem totally absorbed in drama and partying. Many adults live as though identity comes from a career. Happiness supposedly means having a nice house and a new car every three years. But maybe you've seen adults who do nothing but work, complain, and seem unhappy. You may even have seen supposedly "successful" adults who treat each other poorly, or who seem incapable of loving relationships. The messages from social media and entertainment are just as unclear.

The world contains many blessings, but people are often confused about the most important issues. What makes a person matter? What makes a person happy? Does being confident mean dating as much as possible? Does being attractive mean showing off your body or flirting with everyone? If you listen to the world, it's easy to conclude that you are worth nothing more than how good you look, how well you perform, and how much you own.

But there's so much more to the story. God—the one who made you a unique and unrepeatable masterpiece—loves you too much to leave you feeling lost in the world! God made you who you are. He knows where you're going and will show you how to get there.

IF YOU ASK ME ...

- *Someone who is a good example of a free, happy person is* _____.

- *Social media often defines happiness and freedom as* _____.

The whole journey centers on Jesus, who is the ultimate example of how to be fully human. At the **Incarnation,** God the Son became one of us. He took on a body like ours and experienced the same challenges and struggles that we do. He lived as we do, walking, talking, eating, sleeping, praying, teaching, healing. Jesus reveals what it really means to be human and shows us how to live a fully free human life that leads to true happiness.

Then, in his Passion and death, Jesus showed us what love really is. Even though he was totally innocent, Jesus did not run from the Cross. Our sins may have nailed him to the Cross, but his love for us held him there. Jesus' death and Resurrection are proof that God is a Father who loves us and keeps his promises.

God also shows us the way by inspiring holy men and women with wisdom that they can share. We know these holy people as the **saints**. God inspired St. John Paul II with answers to those deep questions about identity and happiness.

St. John Paul II was a man who truly loved young people. He understood how difficult it can be to find the truth when media, entertainment, and society surround you with mistaken ideas. In a collection of talks called the **Theology of the Body**, St. John Paul II addressed the big questions we've been asking: *Who am I? Where am I going? How do I get there?*

The Theology of the Body reveals how our visible bodies express the truth about our invisible souls—and even how our bodies can reflect God's invisible love. The Theology of the Body also teaches many things about our relationships with God and others.

This program will help you discover the good news that God inspired St. John Paul II to share:

- You are a son or daughter of God, made in his image and likeness.

- You have been created for loving relationships with God and others.

- You have the freedom to choose how you will live your life. Knowing our full human story helps us choose the path to happiness in this life and ultimately in heaven.

- Our human relationships help us understand the relationship of the Holy Trinity: the one God, three Persons (the Father, the Son, and the Holy Spirit) who love each other eternally.

You can enter this part of your life confident and excited about who you are and who you will become. You can have good, close friendships. You can have peaceful relationships with those of the other sex.

God knows you and loves you even more than you know and love yourself. Trust him to offer you a plan far better than mere popularity, money, or power. God also offers you a map. Most important of all, he gives you Jesus to be your guide and friend along the way.

Are you ready to go?

IF YOU ASK ME ...

- *The big question I am most excited to answer is* _____.

  » Who am I?

  » Where am I going?

  » How do I get there?

Quick Quiz

1. The first key question is "_____ are you?"

2. Human persons are made in God's _____ and _____.

3. You are a _____ of God.

4. As human persons, we have deep desires for _____ and happiness.

5. God created us with these desires so that we would look for him, find him, and freely _____ to love him.

6. At the _____, God the Son chose to become one of us.

7. Jesus reveals to us what it means to live a fully free human life that leads to true _____.

8. The _____ of the _____ reveals how our visible bodies express the truth about our invisible souls.

 Video 3: Witness and Wrap-Up

A Gift of Self

God created you, unique and unrepeatable, as a gift to the world! How can you make a gift of yourself to others?

Decorate the outline of the hand below to reflect your own personality. On each finger, write one way to give of yourself to the following people:

- Thumb: Your family
- Pointer finger: Your teachers
- Middle finger: Your friends
- Ring finger: Your church parish
- Little finger: Your community

Got It?

Remember these three big questions. Remember them when you get busy or bored or distracted. They are the questions that the Theology of the Body will help you to explore and answer.

- Who are you?
- Where are you going?
- How are you going to get there?

CLOSING PRAYER

+ In the name of the Father, and of the Son, and of the Holy Spirit. Amen.

In the divine image, Lord, you created him; male and female you created them. Lord, you made each of us to be a gift. Help us remember the gift of our identity as your beloved sons and daughters. Help us trust and follow you to the happiness our hearts long for.

Jesus, you gave us your Mother Mary to be our mother on our journey to heaven, so we pray, *Hail Mary* ... Amen.

VOCABULARY

human person: God created human persons in his image and likeness for our own sake—just so he could love us and we could return that love. Every human person is made unique and unrepeatable, male or female, with a body and soul.

Incarnation: The Incarnation refers to Jesus, who is fully God, becoming fully man. God the Son became man to reveal the truth of our humanity and save us from the destruction caused by sin.

saint: A saint is someone who has lived a holy life, practiced virtue to a heroic degree, and chosen to love God above all things. Saints come from every place, ethnicity, circumstance, and background. Saints may be priests or nuns, married, single, or even children. The Catholic Church canonizes (gives the title "Saint" to) these holy people to offer us examples of how we, too, should live. We are all called to live holy lives.

Theology of the Body: On Wednesdays from 1979 to 1984, St. John Paul II gave talks about how the human body reveals that human persons are created male and female in the image of God, with freedom for loving relationships and called to make a gift of ourselves on our way to happiness in heaven. These teachings are known as the Theology of the Body.

Lesson Two: Our Story

GOD'S PLAN, SIN, AND A SAVIOR

OPENING PRAYER

+ In the name of the Father, and of the Son, and of the Holy Spirit. Amen.

In the divine image, Lord, you created him; male and female you created them. Father, you call us to be like you, and you have given us all we need to be happy. Help us never forget that you have rescued us and set us free through the life, death, and Resurrection of your Son, Jesus.

Jesus, you taught us to address your Father as you did, and so,
in the Holy Spirit we pray, *Our Father … Amen.*

"We come from God, we depend on God, God has a plan for us—a plan for our lives, for our bodies, for our souls, for our future. This plan for us is extremely important—so important that God became man to explain it to us."

—St. John Paul II, Address to Young People, New Orleans, 1987

THE BIG PICTURE

Has an older relative ever told you a story about when you were little? You might have learned details that you had remembered incorrectly. Maybe you learned new information that you never knew before. Learning the full story helps you fully understand yourself.

As God's sons and daughters, we need to know our full human story so we understand who we are, where we're headed, and how to get there. When St. John Paul II saw humanity forgetting our full human story, he set out to remind us through the Theology of the Body. Our full human story includes God's beautiful original plan for us, our dramatic fall as we turned away from God in sin, and the triumph of Jesus in rescuing us from darkness and opening the way for us back to the eternal light of heaven.

When we know our full human story, we can learn how to live in the freedom and happiness that we really want and that God wants for us.

Let's go to the beginning.

STORY STARTER

When I was five, my mom took me shopping to buy a gift for my friend Matthew's birthday. His big party was the next day, and I had been thinking about it all week. Like all five-year-olds, I loved birthday parties: games, friends, and that cake-and-ice-cream sugar high. I couldn't wait!

To buy his gift, we went to our local toy shop. It wasn't a big box store with a toy department stuffed behind groceries and household items. This shop sold nothing but toys. From wall to wall, aisle to aisle, it was packed with games, action figures, dolls, trucks, bikes, costumes, remote control vehicles, even candy—every kid's fantasy.

As I walked down an aisle, something caught my eye: a toy sword, but not just any sword. This sword talked, had flashing lights, and looked exactly like the sword that superheroes used to defeat evil villains in the movies. I instantly forgot about Matthew.

"Mom!" I yelled awkwardly. "Look at this sword! I need it! Can we get it? It's what I've always wanted!"

As mothers sometimes must, she burst my bubble. "Honey, remember why we're here. Tomorrow is Matthew's birthday. We're here to

shop for him. You can get a toy for yourself some other day."

I couldn't let it go. "But Mom!" I persisted. "I NEED IT!"

Then I threw an outrageous tantrum right there in the middle of the store. As I flailed and screamed on the floor, my mom kept her cool and made a deal with me.

"Okay, I am going to give you a choice. You can get the sword. But if you do, you can't go to Matthew's party because you won't have a gift. And you will have to call and tell him why you can't come."

She's bluffing, I thought. Without hesitation, I snatched the sword and raced to the checkout to seal the deal. The sword would be mine, all mine!

My mom looked disappointed, but she kept her word. She paid the cashier and silently walked me back to the car. I gripped the sword and fantasized about all the cool stuff I could do with it. But as she buckled me in, something clicked deep inside me. Maybe she hadn't been bluffing after all.

"Uh, Mom? Do I really have to skip the party?"

She answered firmly, "Yep. That's what you chose."

The words hit me hard. I asked, "Do I really have to call Matthew?"

"Yes. That was the deal."

Then the real crying started: hot tears, followed by runny snot and loud sobbing. "I don't want the sword anymore!" I wailed. "I want to go to Matthew's party! I take it back!"

But my choice had been made. My mom had tried to help me see that choosing the sword was a bad deal. She knew that being selfish would only cheat me. I would hurt my friend's feelings and end up alone.

That afternoon I called Matthew to tell him I had chosen a plastic sword over him. A week later, as I played alone in the backyard, the cheap plastic sword broke apart. In the end, I had nothing to show for my selfish choice. —*Colin MacIver*

IF YOU ASK ME ...

- *One of the best parties I ever went to was _____.*

- *One time I chose to _____ when I should have chosen to _____.*

- *Something I really wanted that later disappointed me was _____.*

Video 1: Introduction

IF YOU ASK ME ...

- *How do you feel when you are tricked or scammed? _____*

_____

Video 2: To the Core

VIDEO QUESTIONS

1. **True or False:** Knowing who we are means knowing our story.

2. **True or False:** Sin and death were a part of God's original plan for humanity.

3. **True or False:** Jesus shows us what a fully human life can look like.

A big problem

We all want to be happy, but we have a big problem: **sin**. Why is sin bad? How does sin hurt our happiness?

Happiness comes from choosing what is really good. The greatest good is love. God's laws show us what is really good and how to love. The more we choose to love God and others, the happier we will be. Sin is the opposite, and it has the opposite effect. When we choose not to follow God's laws, we are choosing something less than what is truly good.

Sin distracts us into thinking that we know better than God. We lose sight of our true identity, relationships, and mission. When we sin, we fall for the lie that something we want will make us happier than loving God and others. We think sin will give us pleasure,

fun, or freedom. But sin is a scam. Sin never delivers what it promises. The temptation to sin is a trick designed to lead us into destruction.

Sin is like choosing the plastic sword instead of our friends, and now we're alone in the backyard with a broken toy.

When we choose ourselves over everything else, we always miss the mark. We may feel a moment of pleasure, but it doesn't last. Selfishness is miserable. Have you ever met someone who was both really selfish *and* really happy?

Sometimes we experience how sin backfires. We feel regret and want to take things back. Yet we still find ourselves slipping again into temptation.

Even when we know sin will hurt us, we choose it because it seems so desirable in the moment. We make excuses and tell ourselves it's not a big deal. Even when we know sin will hurt others, we convince ourselves that it's okay.

God did not make us for this mess.

In the beginning, God created the first human persons free from sin, to be fully free to live his plan of love and happiness. They knew who they were and what their purpose was. Before sin, they didn't experience the tug of sin that we experience now. So what happened?

In the beginning

Before anything else existed, God was there. God did not need anything or anyone else because God *is* love. The Holy Trinity is three truly distinct divine Persons—Father, Son, and Holy Spirit—who have loved each other freely for all eternity. God is complete in himself.

> ## IF YOU ASK ME …
>
> • *God is* _____. *(Write the first word that comes to your mind.)*

Yet God's love is so great that he wants to share it. In the beginning, he created the first human persons: a man and woman called Adam and Eve. God made them **in his image and likeness** for their own sake. This means that God made Adam and Eve just so he could love them and so they could return that love. When Adam and Eve freely loved one another, they reflected the love of the Trinity.

God gave Adam and Eve a perfect paradise. Imagine! No insecurity. No drama. No family problems, no anxiety, no wondering whether they belonged. They lived in peace, security, and freedom. They knew God was the source of all the good in their lives. They could not have asked

for—or even imagined—anything better than what God gave them. All they needed to do was continue trusting God to provide and allow him to reveal the fullness of their human identity.

God's desire was for Adam and Eve to love him and each other. Because love must be freely chosen, God gave them the freedom to choose. Love is not possible without choice. You cannot force someone to love you, and nobody can make you love him or her. You have probably experienced this reality with something much less significant than love. Maybe you have been pushed to try a hobby or eat a food that you just didn't like. No amount of pushing can make you like something you don't. If it's impossible to force people to like hobbies or food, it is even more impossible to force love. Love is not love at all unless it is freely chosen and freely given.

The disaster of sin

God gave Adam and Eve **free will** (the ability to choose) to make love possible. But free will also means we can choose *not* to love. Free will allows us to choose either right *or* wrong, good *or* evil.

As a loving Father, God wanted his children to be happy and fulfilled. He knew **Satan** would try to take advantage of Adam and Eve's free will and tempt them to choose wrong. God did not want them to suffer the misery that sin would bring, so he prepared Adam and Eve to face temptation. God warned them that sin would hurt them. It wasn't a trick or a test; God was like a parent protecting a child by warning, "If you touch that hot stove, you'll burn your hand!" If Adam and Eve used their free will to choose what was wrong, they would die (Genesis 2:17).

Sure enough, Satan soon tempted Adam and Eve. Like all temptation to sin, this one was a lie. Satan said they shouldn't follow God's rules. He lied and told them that God was only trying to control them. He said they should disobey God and do what they wanted instead.

Adam and Eve had overwhelming evidence that God loved them and had given them rules for their own happiness. Despite this, they fell for Satan's scam. (We call this "the Fall.") They made the selfish choice and disobeyed God. But their sin missed the mark (as sin always does) and failed to satisfy them. And just as God had warned, sin brought disorder and death—not just to Adam and Eve but to the whole human race.

Original Sin

This damage and disorder from Adam and Eve's sin is called **Original Sin**. God designed human nature with the grace of holiness. But Adam and Eve's choice to sin wasted this treasure of grace. Now we live without something that we should have had.

Original Sin is like losing an inheritance. Imagine you were supposed to inherit a huge stack of cash, but then someone set it on fire. Money that has been burned is not misplaced or saved for later; it is simply gone. With our spiritual inheritance gone, we now find it really difficult to overcome sin.

Sin damaged and disordered four different relationships that had been in perfect order:

- **Our relationship with the physical world.** Bodily hardship and suffering began. Instead of having everything we need for our bodies, we struggle to maintain food and shelter. We experience injury, defects, and disease, and someday we all die.

- **Our bodies' relationship with our souls.** Before the Fall, Adam and Eve's bodily actions flowed from their pure souls. But after they sinned, they began to experience a struggle within themselves. After the Fall, their souls didn't have the same purity and clarity, and their bodily actions didn't flow naturally toward the good. This tendency toward sin is called **concupiscence.**

- **Our relationship with each other.** Instead of perfectly loving and accepting each other, Adam and Eve began to experience tension and misunderstanding. They covered their bodies because sin made them feel insecure and ashamed. Don't we still deal with the same issues? We fight with family members, we feel insecure about our looks, we worry about whether we are loved, we fear rejection.

- **Our relationship with God.** Instead of being in total union with God, Adam and Eve cut themselves off from him like a kite cut from its string. God did not stop loving Adam and Eve, but they chose to reject his love, thinking they would find something better. Adam and Eve soon saw that nothing better than God's love exists, because everything good comes from his love.

Original Sin triggered an immediate cycle that we all recognize. We aim for real freedom and happiness, but we miss the mark entirely with sin. We misuse our free will to choose what's wrong instead of love. We choose the toy sword instead of our friends. We end up unsatisfied. How do we find again what God gave us in the beginning? How do we find what we really want?

> *We aim for real **freedom** and **happiness**, but we miss the mark entirely with sin.*

Satisfied hearts

Do you ever crave a specific food, like ice cream, but you don't have any in the freezer? Searching for a substitute, you stand there with the fridge door open until your mom yells at you to stop air-conditioning the whole house. Maybe yogurt will do. It's creamy and sweet like ice cream, right? One bite, though, and the substitute fails. Now you want ice cream more than ever! The more you try to substitute for what you *really* crave, the more intense the craving gets.

Our hearts deeply crave purpose, happiness, and love. You can probably guess that when God made Adam and Eve, these desires were totally satisfied by their closeness to God and to each other. But when sin disordered our experience, we lost sight of how to satisfy our restless hearts.

What do craving hearts do? They try to find substitutes for what they really want. They try one thing after another, but nothing really hits the target. The world offers all kinds of substitutes. Just consider the ads trying to convince us that some product will make us happy and satisfied. But is that reality? New stuff gives us excitement for a moment, but then the excitement washes away and our hearts are still searching.

So what really strikes the bullseye of our hearts? The answer: a joy that never ends!

IF YOU ASK ME ...

- *When I crave _____, having _____ instead is an unfulfilling substitute.*

- *It seems like many people wrongly think _____ will satisfy their craving for love.*

Ultimate destiny

How often do you even think about heaven?

In our search for freedom and happiness, heaven is our ultimate destiny. Jesus' victory over death changed everything. Real happiness and satisfaction are possible. We are not doomed to sin and misery. We can choose to resist sin and seek grace. Our hearts can be satisfied, but God's plan is even bigger than happiness in this life. God's plan for us is for joy that never ends.

Every earthly good points us to the ultimate joy of heaven. Why is ice cream so good, and why do we crave it? Because the goodness of ice cream gives us a tiny hint about the goodness of God and heaven! Why are we sad when our spoons hit the bottom of the carton? Because pleasure reminds us of something even more satisfying that we haven't reached yet. Why are sunrises so beautiful? Because they reflect God's beauty! Why do sunsets make us long for more? Because they remind us of something even more beautiful that is still to come.

What's the best reminder on earth of the happiness we will experience in heaven? Love!

Quick Quiz

1. Happiness comes from choosing what is truly _____.

2. In the beginning, God created the first human persons free from _____.

3. Sin causes us to lose sight of our true _____, relationships, and mission.

4. When Adam and Eve freely loved one another, they reflected the love of the _____.

5. God gave Adam and Eve _____, the ability to choose, which makes love possible.

6. The damage and disorder from Adam and Eve's sin are called _____.

7. Sin damaged and disordered four of our relationships: with the physical world, with each other, with God, and between our body and our _____.

8. Our hearts deeply crave purpose, happiness, and _____.

9. In our search for freedom and happiness, _____ is our ultimate destiny.

 Video 3: Witness and Wrap-Up

Restoring What We Lost

Our first parents made a terrible deal with sin. They squandered grace in exchange for ... nothing. We do the same when we sin. But in the Sacrament of Reconciliation, God restores what sin squandered. In Confession, we say an Act of Contrition, which expresses our repentance and our resolve to do better, say yes to God's love, and turn away from the scam of sin. This sacrament restores our souls with grace.

Take a few minutes now to quietly examine your life. What commitments or promises are you finding hard to keep? What do you want to do better? Change is possible, but not on your own! Our weaknesses are the exact places where we need God's grace.

After reflection, with the aid of the Holy Spirit, resolve to do better. Use the words of an Act of Contrition to ask for God's help: I firmly resolve, with the help of your grace, to ... (You can find the Act of Contrition in the Catholic Prayers section on page 133.)

Got It?

Sin doesn't just break a rule, it ruins relationships. With who?

With God, others, nature, and you.

CLOSING PRAYER

+ In the name of the Father, and of the Son, and of the Holy Spirit. Amen.

In the divine image, Lord, you created him; male and female you created them. Lord, you gave us a wonderful plan for living in freedom and unity with creation, ourselves, each other, and you. You are the way, the truth, and the life. Help us say yes to you and no to every scam that temptations to sin offer us. Jesus, you gave us your Mother Mary, who teaches us to be open to your love, and so we pray, *Hail Mary ...* Amen.

VOCABULARY

sin: Sin is the choice not to follow God's laws. When we sin, we do something God says we should not do or we fail to do something God says we should do. Sin is a failure to love God and others.

in his image and likeness: Human persons are created to reflect the love of the Trinity. The Trinity is three Persons in one God—Father, Son, and Holy Spirit—who eternally give themselves to each other in love. We are meant to do the same so that when we are in loving relationships, we understand more about God.

in the beginning: In the Garden of Eden, God created the first human persons fully able to live his plan of happiness for them. The way God originally created Adam and Eve is the way human beings were designed to live.

free will: God created us with the ability to choose so that we are able to love. This ability to choose is necessary because love must be freely chosen and given. God wanted us to love him and each other, so he gave us free will.

Original Sin: Original Sin refers to Adam and Eve's sin and its damaging effect on all of humanity. God designed human nature with the grace of holiness and the ability to choose what is good. Original Sin is the loss of this grace. Original Sin damages our ability to know what is right, choose what is good, and love; it causes us to suffer and even die; and it makes us tend to commit sin, even when we try not to.

concupiscence: After the loss of grace in Original Sin, we have a tendency toward sin and selfishness. This tendency is caused by our damaged desires, which are called concupiscence.

Satan: Satan was an angel who rejected God's will. He became the enemy of love and tempted Adam and Eve to sin. He is called "the father of lies" because he tempts us to sin with false promises of happiness.

Lesson Three: Me, Myself, and I
THE BODY AND THE SOUL

OPENING PRAYER

+ In the name of the Father, and of the Son, and of the Holy Spirit. Amen.

In the divine image, Lord, you created him; male and female you created them.
Father, thank you for the sacred gifts of our bodies and souls. Thank you for sending your Son to save us and show us how to live. Help us to always glorify you in our bodies, as men and women who live and love as you taught us.

Jesus, you taught us to address your Father as you did, and so,
in the Holy Spirit, we pray, *Our Father ...* Amen.

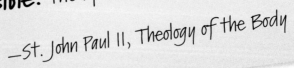

"The body, and only the body, is capable of making visible what is invisible: the spiritual and the divine."

—St. John Paul II, Theology of the Body

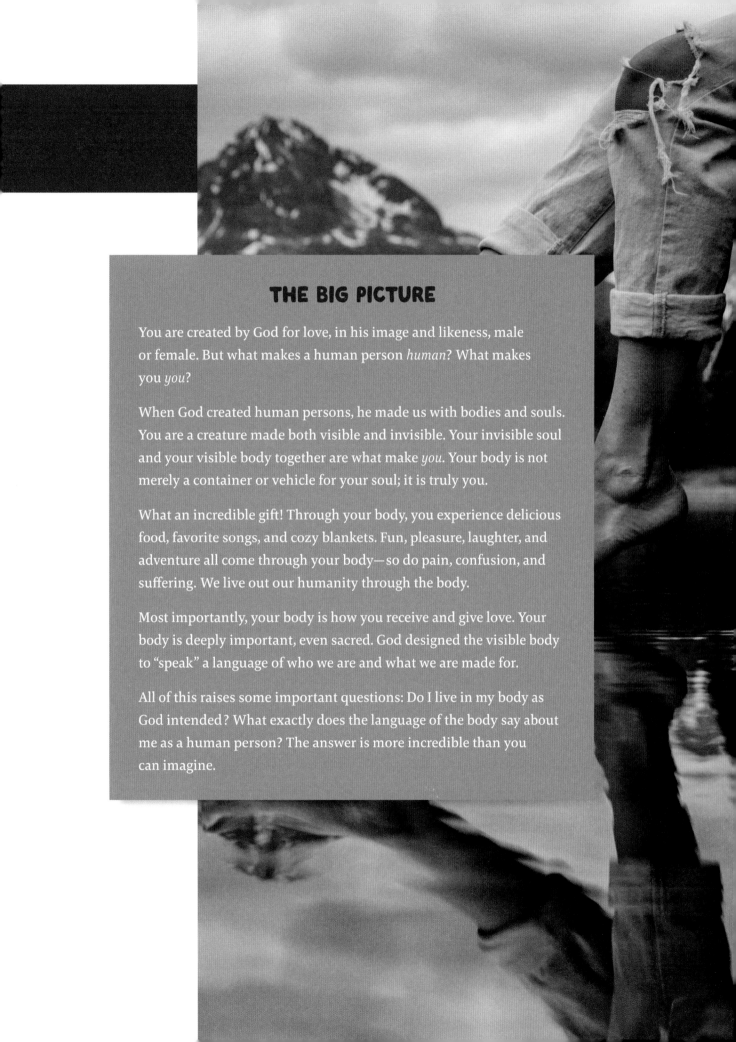

THE BIG PICTURE

You are created by God for love, in his image and likeness, male or female. But what makes a human person *human*? What makes you *you*?

When God created human persons, he made us with bodies and souls. You are a creature made both visible and invisible. Your invisible soul and your visible body together are what make *you*. Your body is not merely a container or vehicle for your soul; it is truly you.

What an incredible gift! Through your body, you experience delicious food, favorite songs, and cozy blankets. Fun, pleasure, laughter, and adventure all come through your body—so do pain, confusion, and suffering. We live out our humanity through the body.

Most importantly, your body is how you receive and give love. Your body is deeply important, even sacred. God designed the visible body to "speak" a language of who we are and what we are made for.

All of this raises some important questions: Do I live in my body as God intended? What exactly does the language of the body say about me as a human person? The answer is more incredible than you can imagine.

STORY STARTER

My family could have paid rent at church—that's how often my parents made us go. We went to Sunday Mass, of course, and then again on Tuesday evenings. Many weeks we also went back on Fridays for Stations of the Cross. Then there were holy days of obligation and special events like Bible school and youth group.

So it was bound to happen: I would get bored at church. *Really* bored. Hadn't I heard all this before? Didn't the priest say the same prayers at every Mass? Didn't we sing the same songs every time? Sometimes I was so bored that I felt jealous of my drooling baby brother, who was still young enough to play with toys during Mass.

That's when the goofing around started. With four siblings, I could always count on at least one of them to join in. We would make paper airplanes out of the church bulletin or try to slam each other's fingers in the hymnal. Before long, my dad would notice.

This was always bad.

Mom and Dad took church very seriously, and we knew it. When our misbehavior caught his attention, Dad lowered his eyebrows and gave us "the look." His **body language** was clear: trouble was in our future. Usually his look was so loaded that we immediately folded our hands and started singing louder than the choir. We did our best to strike a pose that would say, "See, Dad! We're into it! Nothing to see here!"

But if we were too involved in our mischief to notice "the look," Dad would reach his arm down to our level and snap his fingers. Hard. To this day, I still don't know how a snap could sound so intimidating. The snap always worked. We would freeze, look up at Dad's eyebrows, and pray for mercy.

Now my siblings and I are grown. Now we go to church on our own. But sometimes at a family dinner, Dad gives us "the look and the snap" for old times' sake. And even now, that body language has a power that words never could. — *Aimee MacIver*

IF YOU ASK ME ...

- *Give examples of body language in these scenarios:*
    - » I know I'm in trouble when my mom or dad _____.
    - » When my mom or dad _____, I know everything is okay.
    - » My friend always _____ when he or she is _____.

Video 1: Introduction

IF YOU ASK ME ...

- *You can tell when I am feeling _____ because I _____*

_____.

Video 2: To the Core

VIDEO QUESTIONS

1. **True or False:** Men and women experience the world in unique ways.

2. **True or False:** Differences between men and women reveal conflict, not complementarity.

3. **True or False:** Your body is YOU.

The body speaks

Your human body has a special power: it makes visible what is invisible.

Because it reveals a human person, the human body is precious. The value of our bodies doesn't come from how well they perform or how beautiful they look. Our bodies are sacred because *we* are sacred.

IF YOU ASK ME ...

- *I express that I am bored by* _____
  (How do you express boredom with your body?).

- *I express that I am surprised by* _____
  (How do you express surprise with your body?).

- *I think God created the human body to say* _____.

God designed the body to reveal the invisible truths about our human nature, purpose, and destiny. This is what St. John Paul II calls the **language of the body**. This language goes deeper than the surface-level emotions we call "body language." The language of the body speaks the deep truths of God's life in us. It is the love, self-gift, and fidelity that a husband and wife express in marriage, and the language spoken truthfully by celibate men and women who dedicate themselves to loving God with an undivided heart. It is the language of all those who faithfully live the gift of their sexuality according to God's design. And most important, it is the language of Jesus' ultimate sacrifice on the Cross.

Stained glass windows

A human person is not just a soul or just a body, but both. An invisible soul and a visible body are united to create each unique, unrepeatable person. From the moment God created you in your mother's womb, you are soul and body in union. You do not just *have* a soul and a body—you *are* a soul and a body!

Think of a beautiful stained glass window. When the sun shines through it, the window glows with colors and images. But without light, even the most spectacular stained glass window is just a dark, blurry shape. The light reveals the window's true beauty.

But did you know that light on its own is invisible? We can see light only if an object reflects it. When light shines through a stained glass window, the window allows the light to be seen. If there were no window to reflect it, we could never know the light was there. The window and the light are distinct, but they need each other to be fulfilled.

Our souls are like light, and our bodies are like stained glass windows. Our souls give life to our bodies and reveal our true beauty. In return, our bodies allow our souls to be known. Through the body, we can know each other, we can connect with each other, and—most importantly—we can love.

A plan to restore

Sin was a catastrophe for the language of the body. Because of Original Sin, we confuse the true meaning and value of the body. Sometimes we feel uncomfortable in our bodies. Sometimes we think we would be more lovable if our bodies were different: "If I were prettier or taller or faster, would people like me more?"

Even worse, sin disordered and damaged the relationship between body and soul. We are made for love, and God designed our bodies to fulfill this purpose. But because of sin, we are often tempted to use our bodies to lie and hide and use others. Sin is like something that blocks the light from shining through a stained glass window.

How could God solve this disaster? God is so good and loves us so much that he did not just patch up the damage of sin, like taping over a smashed window with a piece of cardboard. No, God restored and increased the original beauty! God made the window even more spectacular, with an even brighter light to make it shine.

When sin brought death to our bodies and souls, God had a plan to restore life. When sin blocked our souls' vision of God, he became visible to our eyes. He chose to speak in the language we understand: the language of the body.

God himself became man, with a human body and soul.

Jesus: true God and true man

Sometimes we forget how incredible the truth is. God the Father invited Mary to become the mother of the Savior. When Mary said yes, she became pregnant through the miraculous power of the Holy Spirit. At the moment of the Incarnation, God the Son took on a human nature, including a human body and soul, which are united to his divine nature in his one divine Person. Somewhere in Bethlehem, the newborn baby crying in Mary's arms was true God and true man.

Imagine what this really means! God, who is all-powerful, became totally vulnerable—a baby in a human family. God, who knows everything, learned to crawl. God, who inspired the writing of the Bible, was taught to write his own name.

In all of history, Jesus is unique. God didn't merely put on a human body like a costume and pretend to go through human life: he truly experienced it the same way you do. He was eleven, twelve, and thirteen years old. He dealt with his voice changing and finding a group of friends. He loved people, felt sad, experienced joy, got angry, cried, and even faced temptation. He went through the same, sometimes difficult, process of growing up that you're going through now.

When was Jesus sad? Lonely? Afraid? The Gospels show us Jesus' full humanity. Read Mark 14:33–34, Luke 10:21, Mark 3:4–5, John 11:35, Mark 10:21, and Hebrews 4:15 to better understand how Jesus shared the same experiences you have.

The Incarnation changes everything

Why is it such a big deal that the Son of God became human? It all comes back to the language of the body:

- **Jesus' human body makes visible God's love.** Sin darkened our vision of God's love, but Jesus' human body made it visible again in an ultimate way. On the Cross, Jesus did the same thing he did at the Last Supper when he said the words we now hear at Mass. He stretched out his hands and said, "This is my body, which is given for you" (Luke 22:19). In other words, "I love you totally, with all that I am."

- **Jesus shows us what our humanity is supposed to look like.** How does your reflection in water compare to your reflection in a mirror? In water, you can see shapes and colors, but the image isn't nearly as clear or accurate as the image in a mirror. We have always been made in God's image. Sin didn't change that, but it blurred the image of who we are and what we are made for. Jesus is like a crystal clear mirror that shows the full truth of what a human person is meant to be. The truth was always there, but our vision was clouded by sin. Until we looked at Jesus, we couldn't see it clearly.

- **Jesus shows us how to live in our bodies.** Jesus lived his human life totally without sin. That really means *totally*! He never told a white lie, ignored his parents, or allowed hateful thoughts to grow. This doesn't mean he didn't get scared, bored, frustrated, or lonely. But how did he choose to respond? The way Jesus handled the highs and lows of human life is how all human persons should act. He showed us how to live in our bodies and become what we are meant to be—like him.

*"This is my **body**, which is given for you."*

Jesus' body speaks

In some ways, Jesus was a regular guy. He didn't write any great books or build any spectacular monuments. He wasn't super popular or rich. He didn't win a sports championship or sell out concerts. So what did he do?

Jesus did the most extraordinary thing in history. He traded places with us.

Because he was sinless, he deserved none of sin's consequences. Because he is God, he deserved total obedience. Yet he chose the opposite of what he deserved.

Adam and Eve used their freedom to choose selfishness and disobedience, bringing death into the world. Jesus freely chose to be unselfish and obedient, bringing life. By making the opposite choice, Jesus brought about the opposite effect—for all of us.

To restore and reveal the fullness of humanity, Jesus had to destroy sin. If sin is total selfishness, the only way to destroy sin is to be totally unselfish. Love was the only thing that could stop the cycle of sin, so Jesus loved. He sacrificed his own life to save us. Jesus gave himself totally for all of us, even for those who hated him.

Imagine Jesus on the Cross with his arms outstretched. The language of Jesus' body on the Cross says, "Do you want to know how much I love you? This much!" His body shouts, "You are so precious that I think you are worth dying for!"

Jesus' body declares who we really are and what we are meant to be forever.

Made for heaven

What happened after Jesus' family and friends took down his dead body from the Cross? They put him in a grave. They wept. They went home and tried to figure out what to do now that he was gone. But God kept his promises. Death always had won before, but this time death could not defeat life.

Jesus is alive! His body was broken, but at the **Resurrection,** he rose again! For the first time ever, death was not the end of life. For forty days after the Resurrection, Jesus visited his friends, enjoyed meals, and experienced the life of his body again. Then his friends watched him go to heaven at the **Ascension.** Jesus is in heaven right now, not as an invisible spirit or ghost but in his resurrected body. He is not broken but whole and complete. His truly human body is united forever with his soul.

Remember that Jesus' body declares who we really are and what we are meant to be forever. Your destiny is not just to grow up, have a career,

> *Jesus is in heaven **right now**, not as an invisible spirit or ghost but in his **resurrected body**. He is not broken but **whole** and **complete**.*

become old, and die. You have so much more to look forward to than just eighty or ninety years on earth. Your destiny is the destiny of Jesus.

Here and now, God wants us to live with heaven as our goal. The little things we do—like helping out at home, backing off in arguments with our parents, or defending someone who is being teased—are ways we can do this.

The more you know Jesus, the more you know who you are. In knowing him, you know that you are destined—body and soul—for heaven.

Quick Quiz

1. The human person is both body and _____.

2. The human body makes visible what is _____.

3. Body language makes visible our inner thoughts and _____.

4. One reason the _____ is so precious is that it reveals a human person.

5. God the Son became man with a human _____ and _____.

6. Jesus shows us what our _____ is supposed to look like.

7. Jesus' human body makes visible _____ love.

8. Three days after he died on the Cross, Jesus _____ from the dead.

9. Our bodies and souls will be reunited in _____.

 Video 3: Witness and Wrap-Up

Body of Christ

The language of Jesus' body didn't end when he ascended to heaven after his Resurrection. It continues through his Church. Because we are body-souls and the language of the body is so important, Jesus left us many visible signs to bring his love and grace into our lives. We call these sacraments.

Sacraments are sensory, meaning that we can see, touch, smell, hear, and even taste God's goodness through our bodies. We don't just think about Christ's Body; in the Eucharist, we really consume his Body and drink his Blood. We don't just think we are sorry and hope we are forgiven; in Reconciliation, we confess our sins and experience God's healing through the priest's words and actions. How cool is that? Think about how your own body participates in the sacraments. Which of your five senses are used in each sacrament?

1. Baptism: _____

2. Eucharist: _____

3. Confirmation: _____

4. Reconciliation: _____

5. Anointing of the Sick: _____

6. Matrimony: _____

7. Holy Orders: _____

Got It?

- *The face of Jesus Christ is the face of true humanity.*

- *Bodies and souls unite
like stained glass windows and light!*

CLOSING PRAYER

(adapted from Psalm 139)

+ In the name of the Father, and of the Son, and of the Holy Spirit. Amen.

In the divine image, Lord, you created him; male and female you created them. O Lord, you know me: you know when I sit and when I stand; you understand my thoughts. Truly you have formed my inmost being; you knit me in my mother's womb. I give you thanks that I am fearfully, wonderfully made; wonderful are your works.

Jesus, your Mother Mary reminds us of God's goodness as well as our own, so we pray, *Hail Mary ...* Amen.

VOCABULARY

body language: Gestures and expressions that communicate inner thoughts and feelings.

language of the body: The major Theology of the Body teaching is that the human body makes visible what is invisible. The body speaks a language without words about our human nature, purpose, and destiny. Jesus shows us that the body reveals a call to total self-gift.

Resurrection: After his death on the Cross, Jesus rose from the dead. His human body and soul were reunited. Jesus' Resurrection opened for us the possibility of resurrection, when our own bodies and souls will reunite after death.

Ascension: After the Resurrection, Jesus literally went up (ascended) body and soul to heaven. He is in heaven now in a constant offering of love. One day, he will return to the earth again in glory to bring us to live with him forever.

OPENING PRAYER

+ In the name of the Father, and of the Son, and of the Holy Spirit. Amen.

In the divine image, Lord, you created him; male and female you created them. Father, thank you for the freedom to become fully the sons and daughters you made us to be. Give us faith, hope, and love to help us accept your invitation to choose what *is* good instead of what only feels good.

Jesus, you remind us who we are and how we should act. Help us approach the Father as you did, as we pray, *Our Father* ... Amen.

"It is Jesus who stirs in you the desire to do something great with your lives, the will to follow an ideal, the refusal to allow yourselves to be ground down by mediocrity, the courage to commit yourselves humbly and patiently to improving yourselves and society, making the world more human and more fraternal."

—St. John Paul II, World Youth Day, Rome, 2000

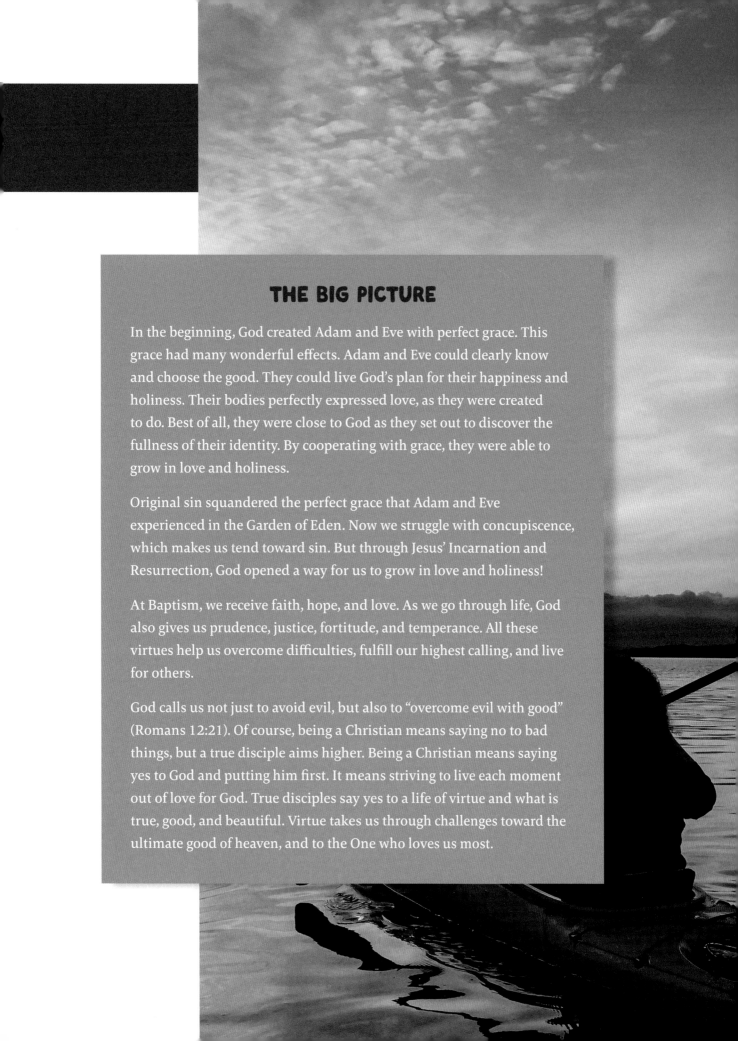

THE BIG PICTURE

In the beginning, God created Adam and Eve with perfect grace. This grace had many wonderful effects. Adam and Eve could clearly know and choose the good. They could live God's plan for their happiness and holiness. Their bodies perfectly expressed love, as they were created to do. Best of all, they were close to God as they set out to discover the fullness of their identity. By cooperating with grace, they were able to grow in love and holiness.

Original sin squandered the perfect grace that Adam and Eve experienced in the Garden of Eden. Now we struggle with concupiscence, which makes us tend toward sin. But through Jesus' Incarnation and Resurrection, God opened a way for us to grow in love and holiness!

At Baptism, we receive faith, hope, and love. As we go through life, God also gives us prudence, justice, fortitude, and temperance. All these virtues help us overcome difficulties, fulfill our highest calling, and live for others.

God calls us not just to avoid evil, but also to "overcome evil with good" (Romans 12:21). Of course, being a Christian means saying no to bad things, but a true disciple aims higher. Being a Christian means saying yes to God and putting him first. It means striving to live each moment out of love for God. True disciples say yes to a life of virtue and what is true, good, and beautiful. Virtue takes us through challenges toward the ultimate good of heaven, and to the One who loves us most.

STORY STARTER

As I ripped off shreds of Christmas wrapping paper, my heart started beating faster. The shape of the box was right. Could it be … ? Finally? I tore off a huge piece, and there it was: my first REAL guitar! I was flat-out in love with a Japanese Fender Stratocaster made especially for left-handers like me.

I had wanted to play guitar for as long as I could remember, but Mom had always said, "Piano lessons first." I hated playing piano. All those practice drills killed me. I wanted to be a rock star! So that Christmas morning was a victory. I plugged in my guitar, threw the strap over my shoulder, and … suddenly realized I had no idea how to play it. Not quite rock-star material yet.

Wisely, Mom had given me another gift: guitar lessons. At my first lesson, I met my teacher, who had huge '80s hair and smelled like he preferred rock and roll to showers. Still, he played guitar like a genius. He promised that he could teach me if I followed his instructions.

I sat down with my new guitar, expecting him to show me all his moves. Instead, he showed me how to hold a guitar and play a few notes—and then he assigned drills for homework. I was disappointed. He was making guitar as pointless and boring as the old piano lessons: nothing but practice over and over instead of my rock-and-roll dream.

But I obeyed. I repeated the drills and found they were pretty hard. That first week, my fingertips grew sore from strumming the sharp guitar strings. Then came painful blisters. I still kept going because I just wanted to be a guitar player and was willing to do whatever it took.

The next week, my instructor taught me more boring drills and a few chords. The week after that, though, he showed me how the chords I had been practicing formed a famous rock song. I'll never forget the moment it all came together. All along I had been learning—bit by bit, week after week—the ingredients to a really cool song.

My sense of rhythm needed work, so I played every day for hours. Then I decided I wanted to sing and play at the same time. I gradually got better. Eventually, I found myself playing and singing at coffee houses, cafés, local concerts, youth group events, weddings, and church.

How did I go from a guy goofing off with drills to someone who gets paid to play and sing? I had to correct my initial understanding of what makes a truly great guitar player. It isn't fame or wealth or selling out concerts. The only real way to become a great guitar player is to play the guitar—a lot. Drill by boring drill. One chord at a time. Otherwise known as practice.—*Colin MacIver*

IF YOU ASK ME ...

- *I had to practice _____ really hard so that I could _____.*

- *I don't like practicing _____, but it's worth it because _____.*

- *One day I want to be a _____, so I will have to practice _____.*

Video 1: Introduction

IF YOU ASK ME ...

- *What is a goal you would like to accomplish? Name a few steps you are going to take to help you achieve your goal.* _____

_____

_____

Video 2: To the Core

VIDEO QUESTIONS

1. **True or False:** A virtue is a firm habit towards something good.

2. **True or False:** The virtue of temperance gives us the courage and strength to do what is hard.

3. **True or False:** The theological virtues are gifts from God.

THE CORE

Time to practice

What do a gold-medal-winning athlete, a museum-worthy artist, and an honor-roll student have in common? It's the same thing that a great rock guitarist, an Oscar-winning actor, and a computer game champ have in common. To become who they want to be, those who excel work and practice hard.

You've heard the saying "Practice makes perfect." Parents say it when they tell you to remake your bed neatly. Teachers or coaches say it when you complain about solving math problems or running drills for the millionth time. Sometimes practice is so boring and repetitive that you might even wonder, *What's the point of this?*

Then you get a good test grade or win a tough soccer match. And you realize that to become who you want to be, you have to practice.

You've already learned a lot about who you are meant to be. You are a son or a daughter of God, made in his image and likeness. Your body speaks a language about love and self-gift. Sin brought damage and disorder to creation, but Jesus gives us hope and a plan. Jesus perfectly lived his humanity to show you, too, how to live. Your ultimate destiny is eternal life in heaven.

All this knowledge is very important because it shows each of us how to be a free, happy, loving human person. But it's not enough just to know these truths. You must practice them. Even if you knew everything about guitars, that knowledge alone wouldn't make you a guitarist. In the same way, just *knowing* who you are meant to be isn't enough. You have to turn that knowledge into practice.

It's not easy. We are surrounded by distractions that block us from knowing the truth and gobble up the time we need to practice it. We try to cover up our true selves with all kinds of social masks. We do, say, and watch things that oppose human dignity because we want to look cool. When we sin, we choose selfishness instead of love and self-gift. We end up doing what Adam and Eve did right after they sinned—we hide ourselves.

And all of this is like training for a marathon by running in circles.

You're becoming mature enough to see how crazy and ineffective it is to run in circles. Maturity means you know the truth and strive to practice it, even if that means making sacrifices. You know who you are as a human person. You know who you are meant to become. You know where you are headed for eternity.

It's time to get real and start running the race.

IF YOU ASK ME ...

• *I know that I should not* _____, *but I do it anyway.*

• *One thing that I know I should do and really want to do is* _____.

Acting human

Why do we arrest someone who vandalizes property but not a dog that chews up furniture? It's because we have a natural sense that, for human beings, some behavior is wrong and some behavior is right. A good person is patient, kind, and truthful. A good person is genuine and works hard. A good person puts others first. We have an instinct for the ideal ways a human person should act and think.

These ideal human behaviors and attitudes are called virtues. A **virtue** is defined as "a strong habit of doing what is good." Virtues are expressed by our visible bodies. We know that the virtue of patience exists because we see people doing whatever they do ... patiently. The same is true of the other virtues.

*You will never be **freer** or **happier** than when you do what is good, because that's what **you** were made for.*

The more we practice virtue, the more truly human we become. Practicing virtue makes us free and happy because it fulfills who we are. A fish will never be freer and happier than when it swims in the ocean, because that's what it was made for. You will never be freer or happier than when you do what is good, because that's what *you* were made for. Original Sin knocks everything out of order, but virtue puts our feelings, thoughts, and reactions back in order, allowing everything to work the way it should. Virtue makes what we do on the outside match who we really are on the inside. Virtue is telling the truth with the language of your body.

Strong habits take practice

A **habit** is something you do frequently, like a routine. The "strong habit" of virtue means doing what is good routinely, not just when it's easy. In fact, virtue grows when you practice it, especially when you don't feel like it! If you are patient only until someone annoys you, then you don't really have a strong habit of patience. The strong habit of patience develops when you choose to be patient even though you *feel* like being impatient.

Virtues are different from other good habits like brushing your teeth. When you practice a virtue in your actions, the habit eventually becomes part of who you are. For example, if you develop the strong habit of telling the truth, you become a more truthful person, and the language of your body matches your truthful heart.

Habits, of course, are developed through practice. You need to practice to become virtuous. Like learning guitar, you do drills even when you don't feel like it. But in the end, when you pick up a guitar, your fingers will just know what to do.

IF YOU ASK ME ...

- *Three virtues I would like to grow in are _____, _____, and _____.*

- *If I _____ every day, I think I can grow in the virtue of _____.*

Kinds of virtue

There are two kinds of virtue: cardinal and theological. The **cardinal virtues** are prudence, justice, fortitude, and temperance. *Cardinal* means "hinge." The cardinal virtues are like hinges that make a door open. When we practice the cardinal virtues, we open the door to other natural virtues as well.

The **theological virtues** are faith, hope, and love. God gives us these virtues at Baptism to lead us to himself. As we grow, we choose to accept and develop them through our thoughts, words, and actions. With faith, we believe in God's love. With hope, we are confident in God's help and his promises. With love, we give the gift of ourselves in relationships.

We always need more growth in faith, hope, and love. Ask God to give you more of these gifts.

The enemy of virtue

Virtue has an enemy: vice. **Vice** is the strong habit of doing what is *not* good. If a strong habit of telling the truth is a virtue, a strong habit of telling lies is a vice.

Vices have the opposite characteristics and effects of virtues. The more you practice a vice, the stronger the bad habit becomes. Just as virtues can become second nature with practice, vices can also become part of your character. For example, the more you give in to using bad language, the more comfortable you will become using bad language. This will eventually make you more comfortable using even worse language.

Being comfortable with vices is like being comfortable in a hungry tiger's den. Even if a vice seems like no big deal at first, all vices are dangerous because they ensnare us in sin.

Habits are like seeds that grow and spread quickly. As plants in a garden grow, they produce new seeds that grow into new plants. Each new plant takes up more garden space. In the space where one plant is growing, another plant can't take root. So virtues produce more goodness and crowd out vices! But vices are deadly because the more evil increases, the less room there is for good.

Vices enslave us and destroy freedom. What happens if you lie? You often need to tell more lies to hide the first one. Soon you're too busy keeping track of the lies to do anything else. Maybe you lied to avoid punishment, but now you're caught in a web and are anything but free.

The battle between virtue and vice can be difficult, so God—who always wants to help us—empowers us with grace.

The gift of grace

Grace is a gift won for us by Jesus' death and resurrection. Grace cranks up your soul with power like spiritual electricity. Without grace, your soul would be lifeless.

Imagine that you are living in the wilderness and trying to start a fire, caveman-style, by rubbing two sticks together. You need perfect weather conditions, a specific kind of stick, and very strong hands. It may take hours to produce a spark, which might or might not grow into a flame. You will probably get some nasty blisters, too. But without fire, you cannot survive, so you have no choice but to keep trying. Much of your time will be spent starting and maintaining your fire.

Now imagine how matches would radically change your life (or a caveman's)! Instant, reliable, powerful fire!

When we accept God's gift of grace, it is like receiving a box of matches in the wilderness. Everything changes. What once seemed almost impossible now becomes possible. The darkness lights up with hope!

Saints and sacraments

We are not alone in the battle of virtue and vice. Thousands of saints are our examples. Male and female. Young and old. Married and single. Priests and nuns. Rich and poor. Popular and outcast. Athletic and artsy. Funny and quiet. Every human person can be a saint, but all saints make the same big choice—they accept God's grace and triumph over vice by practicing virtue.

We receive God's grace through the **sacraments,** especially Reconciliation and the Eucharist. The sacraments are visible signs of God's grace working invisibly. In Confession, you see the visible sign of the priest, and you hear the words of absolution; invisibly, silently, your soul is being cleansed of sin! Reconciliation is like a spout that allows grace to flow into your soul as Jesus absolves your sins.

At the Consecration of the Eucharist, the bread and wine become the real Body and Blood of Jesus. When you receive Communion, you don't receive a piece of bread or a symbol. You receive Jesus himself—the same Jesus who died and rose for you! What an incredible gift to be so close to him. The closer you are to Jesus, who showed us how to live in our bodies and always did the virtuous thing, the more grace you will have to do the same.

> *Every human person can be a saint, but all saints make the same big choice—they accept God's grace and triumph over vice by practicing virtue.*

Connected

Look at your body—it's truly amazing. Many different parts are all connected to make one whole body. No body part functions by itself. As a human person, too, you are one whole, with all the parts of your life connected just as the parts of your body are connected. You don't have one self for your friends, a different self for your family, and still another self for church.

But sometimes we act disconnected. Be honest. Do you treat your family in ways you would never treat strangers? Do you post words online that you would never say to someone's face? Do you pretend to like certain shows or music just so no one thinks you're weird?

Virtue means trying to be consistent in all areas of your life. You cannot make progress toward a certain goal if you do other things that undermine the goal. For example, even if you run ten miles every day, you will never win a marathon if you eat nothing but candy. If you want to become your true self, you can't be a different "you" depending on who you're with. Our actions should match who we are and who we want to become.

You are not a random creature wandering the earth. You are a child of God. You are not made to coast through life but to really live! You are made to love others and give yourself like Jesus! Do your actions match this true identity? Or do your actions say that you don't really care about God? Do you forget about God as soon as the church door closes behind you every Sunday?

IF YOU ASK ME ...

- *I do* _____, *which reveals that I am* _____.

The whole you

At your age, it's common to question your faith. Why should you believe in God just because you've been told to? Of course, your family's wisdom matters. But your faith must become your own. How? By studying it, by being open to it, and mostly by living it. We become walkers by walking. We become speakers by speaking. We become followers of God by following God. Choose to believe in God, accept his grace, and follow his commandments. This is how you become a person of virtue and love.

You may fear that you will be labeled or worry that you won't have any fun. Remember that even Jesus himself faced fear and anxiety when he had to do what was virtuous. Sometimes people rejected or made fun of him. Yet he defeated fear and anxiety by choosing love.

God's love will also defeat your fear or anxiety when you strive to choose virtue. God's love is always complete and consistent; it's not divided into parts. It doesn't change depending on who's watching. God doesn't think some people are cooler or more popular or more worthy of love than others. God always loves. You form yourself by what you do. God loves totally, absolutely, constantly—so God *is* love.

You're growing up, moving toward the fullness of your identity. You're ready to start filling in the blanks about who you are. How will you respond?

Quick Quiz

1. _____ makes perfect.

2. _____ is defined as "a strong habit of doing what is good."

3. Every human person can become a _____.

4. Virtue makes us _____ and happy because it fulfills who we are.

5. The _____ virtues are faith, hope, and charity.

6. The _____ virtues are prudence, justice, fortitude, and temperance.

7. _____ enslave us.

8. _____ is like spiritual electricity. It makes virtue possible.

9. We receive God's grace through the _____.

 Video 3: Witness and Wrap-Up

Habit Check

Many things in our daily lives can lead us to either virtue or vice, depending upon how they are used. Look at the items listed below and think about how you use each one. Next to each item, draw a plus sign (+) if you believe your use of each item is leading you to virtue, or draw a minus sign (–) if you believe your use is leading you to vice. This week, pick one item that seems to be leading you to vice and focus on turning the minus to a plus.

- Messaging

- How much time I spend on devices

- Interacting with my family

- Social media apps

- Video/computer gaming

- Paying attention in school

- Being honest with my parents

- Praying

- Homework

- Language

- Weekend activities

- What I watch and listen to online

- My choice of music

Got It?

In the ER (emergency room), doctors treat serious sickness or injury. When you need healing from vice and sin, go to the ER, the two powerful sacraments of the Eucharist and Reconciliation.

E: **"The Eucharist** is the source and summit of the entire Christian life" (CCC 1324). If you want to grow in virtue, go to Mass, where you can receive Jesus, the source of all virtue. You need to go to Mass at least every Sunday. Let the language of your body speak about your inner love for Jesus.

R: **Reconciliation** absolves our sin and gives us the grace to move back toward Jesus. It calls us deeper and deeper into conversion, turning our hearts toward him (CCC 1423). If we commit a mortal sin, we must receive Reconciliation before receiving the Eucharist.

CLOSING PRAYER

+ In the name of the Father, and of the Son, and of the Holy Spirit. Amen.

In the divine image, Lord, you created him; male and female you created them. O Lord, you made me to give the best of myself for the good of others. Help me to accept the gift of your grace so your power may be made perfect in my weakness. Please help me every day to become more like you.

Jesus, your Mother Mary perfectly lived a virtuous life, so we turn to her now as we pray, *Hail Mary* ... Amen.

VOCABULARY

habit: An action repeated so often that it becomes a natural part of a person's character.

virtue: A strong habit of doing what is good. Virtue empowers us to love God and others freely. Virtues are expressed by how we live in our visible bodies.

cardinal virtues: *Cardinal* means "hinge," so the cardinal virtues—prudence, justice, fortitude, and temperance—are like hinges that open the door to other natural virtues as well.

theological virtues: The theological virtues are faith, hope, and love. "Theological" means these virtues are given to us by God and lead us to him.

vice: A strong habit of doing what is not good. Vices enslave us to sin and rob us of the power to love. Even small vices lead to other vices.

grace: God's free gift of divine life in us, which was won for us by Jesus and which we receive especially through the sacraments. Like spiritual electricity for our souls, grace empowers us to live out virtues.

sacrament: Sacraments are visible signs of invisible realities that bring grace to our souls. Sacraments are administered through the Church.

Reconciliation: Also called Confession, the Sacrament of Reconciliation allows us to repent for our sins and have our souls wiped clean. Jesus is the one who absolves our sins; priests are his instruments in Confession. When we confess our sins to a priest, it is like talking directly to Jesus himself.

Eucharist: Also called Holy Communion, the Eucharist is the greatest sacrament because it is literally Jesus himself—Body and Blood, Soul and Divinity. When the priest prays the Consecration at Mass, the bread and wine look the same but they become Jesus himself.

OPENING PRAYER

+ In the name of the Father, and of the Son, and of the Holy Spirit. Amen.

In the divine image, Lord, you created him; male and female you created them. You made each of us unique gifts to the world through being unrepeatable young men and women. Help us to reverence our bodies, accept ourselves, and receive one another as the great gifts you made us to be.

Jesus, you taught us to address your Father as you did—and so, as sons and daughters, brothers and sisters in the Holy Spirit, we pray, *Our Father* ... Amen.

"Only the chaste man and the chaste woman are capable of true love."

—St. John Paul II, *Love and Responsibility*

THE BIG PICTURE

As a kid, maybe you groaned, "Gross!" if you saw a man and a woman kiss. Now, though, you may see members of the other sex as more than just friends. You may develop crushes. Your peers may start talking about dating and who "likes" whom. As your body changes and grows, you may feel really aware of yourself and others as male or female.

From the beginning with Adam and Eve, romantic attraction has been one of the strongest human desires. It's no accident. God created each human person with a male or female body and identity. He created them with differences that draw them together into a wonderful unity. He designed the sexual act that bonds spouses in love and creates new life. God intended all of it to be a powerful sign of his love. In fact, Scripture even says that spousal love reflects the bond of Christ with us, the Church.

Everything around us—shows, music, movies, social media, ads—seems obsessed with romantic attraction and sex. But our culture often distorts God's design for sex. Being male or female is sometimes described as a preference or personal choice rather than an unchanging truth about how God has created us. Men and women are sometimes shown as competitors or enemies. Sex often gets twisted into a source of manipulation, confusion, regret, and shame. Spousal love is rarely discussed as a sign of God's love.

Our Catholic faith offers a higher, more beautiful vision of sex than the world often does. There is a wonderful truth about sex that God wants us to discover, live out, and enjoy.

STORY STARTER

Like many couples, Louis and Zelie Martin met, fell in love, and got married. They wrote love letters when they were apart, helped each other run small businesses to support their family, and worked together as parents of their children. Most importantly, they challenged and encouraged each other to become holy.

Their love was fruitful in so many ways! Louis and Zelie became the first married couple to be canonized together. One of their daughters became a great saint, too: St. Thérèse of Lisieux, who is often called the Little Flower.

Louis and Zelie are an example of the beauty and gift of being male or female. Louis was complete in himself as a man, husband, and father. Zelie was complete in herself as a woman, wife, and mother. Each had a unique personality and gifts. Louis ran a watchmaking business, while Zelie operated a lacemaking company. They were different and distinct—but together, they brought out something wonderful in each other. Their differences, in union, were a wonderful gift for the Church.

Why did God create us male or female? What does it mean to be a man or a woman? St. Louis and St. Zelie are models for us as we enter the mystery.

IF YOU ASK ME ...

- *One stereotype about girls is* _____.

- *One stereotype about boys is* _____.

- *One way girls and boys are genuinely different is* _____.

- *Something I appreciate about girls is* _____.

- *Something I appreciate about boys is* _____.

Video 1: Introduction

IF YOU ASK ME ...

- *What would life be like if the world had only girls? What would life be like if the world had only boys?* _____

_____

_____

Video 2: To the Core

VIDEO QUESTIONS

1. **True or False:** In the Garden of Eden, man and God had original unity.

2. **True or False:** Chastity is a virtue that seeks to control us and keep us away from love.

3. **True or False:** The way you live and love right now is preparing you for God's plan for your life.

Created male and female

What is sex? If you answered that sex is a physical act to express **spousal** love and create new life, you would be correct! But sex is also something we *are*. St. John Paul II said sex first refers to our identity as male or female.

We can see that male and female bodies have clear differences. These bodily differences are necessary for the act of sex, which allows husband and wife to unite their bodies in a free, total, faithful way that can create new life. These bodily differences between male and female reveal a call to communion and self-gift.

It is not just their bodies that make men and women different. They are also different in how they relate to God, each other, and the world. We can often observe different tendencies or traits displayed by men and women, but these patterns do not define your sex. What

if you're a girl who feels like you don't share the tendencies of most girls? What if you're a boy who feels like you don't share the tendencies of most boys?

Being male or female doesn't mean we live by rigid stereotypes. Being male or female is not about a preference, a feeling, or what we like to do. Our maleness or femaleness is revealed by the male or female bodies we receive from God. It is not defined by how you like to dress, your personality traits, your hobbies, or who your friends are.

Being a man or woman doesn't change depending on these things, either. At conception, when your body was one single cell, that cell was already marked as male or female. Even as you grow now, the trillions of cells that make up your body are all stamped as male or female. Our maleness or femaleness is essential to our identity—and you can be confident that God created you intentionally to be his unique, unrepeatable son or daughter.

*Our maleness or femaleness is **essential** to our identity*

Some people compare men and women, depicting them as competitors or threats to each other. Some suggest that we should erase or deny differences between the sexes. But these views reflect a huge lack of understanding. Men and women are great gifts to one another! The world thrives when, instead of comparing, competing, or erasing, we welcome the gift of being male or female as God made us to be—and welcome the gift of the other sex.

Complementarity

After God created Adam, he said, "It is not good that the man should be alone" (Genesis 2:18). Adam himself was good, but his aloneness was a problem. God presented many creatures to Adam, but none of them was an equal partner. So God put Adam into a deep sleep and finished his masterpiece: Eve. She was formed from Adam's own self, so she was an equal. When Adam saw Eve for the first time, he exclaimed in joy, "This at last is bone of my bones and flesh of my flesh!" (Genesis 2:23). God proclaimed that the happily married couple together was *very* good (Genesis 1:31).

God created man and woman in his image, equal in dignity to each other while also unique. In our female or male bodies, we live out this image in singular ways that, together, reflect the fullness of God. This reality is called **complementarity**. It means that each sex reflects God in a way that the other sex cannot. The unique differences of men and women do several things:

- They show each sex's unique goodness.
- They reveal our call to communion and self-gift.

Because of the differences,

- Men and women bring out the best in each other.
- Women and men grow to a full flourishing in motherhood and fatherhood (spiritual, biological, or both).

Complementarity doesn't mean that, on their own, men and women are incomplete or missing something. We are not one half waiting for another half to be complete. Instead, complementarity means that our differences make our unique goodness as human persons shine even brighter.

Sex says self-gift

As human persons, Adam and Eve were made to express their invisible gift of self through the visible gift of their bodies. As male and female, their bodily differences enabled them to give their bodies to each other in the physical act of sex. Sex says, "I give myself totally to you." By God's design, the act of sex is a gift that holds a married couple close in love and creates new life.

Because God made man and woman in his image, all parts of a husband and wife's relationship—including sex—participate in that image. The three Persons of the Trinity make a loving self-gift to each other for eternity. A husband and a wife reflect this mystery by making a loving self-gift to each other for the rest of their lives. The spouses' constant love for each other reflects the constant love between the Father, the Son, and the Holy Spirit. Marriage is a human sign of the Trinity's ultimate love. Marriage and sex are good and holy because God created them to reflect divine love.

IF YOU ASK ME ...

Circle the action that in your opinion is most appropriate for the relationship and situation being described.

1. Grandma comes over for dinner.

   Fist bump   Kiss on the cheek   High five   Genuflect

2. You see your uncle in the grocery store.

   Curtsey   Handshake   Hug   Wink from across the aisle

3. The bishop comes to your classroom.

   Wink   Genuflect   High five   Stand when he enters the room

4. Your best friend gets bad news.

   High five   Hand on shoulder   Hug   Head butt

Shame and nakedness

Naked. Even the word sometimes makes us giggle. Our natural reaction to nakedness is often embarrassment and an urge to cover up. But Genesis tells us that in the beginning, Adam and Eve were naked without shame.

Shame is the urge we have to cover up or hide something from God, others, and maybe even ourselves. Shame is about guilt, fear, and vulnerability. You might feel shame when you do something wrong. You might also feel shame when you are "overexposed" physically or emotionally. What if you did something silly at home that your parents later told everyone about? You might feel shame or want to hide because something private was exposed, and you felt vulnerable.

In the beginning, Adam and Eve had no sense of shame. God created them in love and gave them a paradise to live in. They had no insecurities to make them feel like they had to hide personal things from each other or from God. They did not use each other. Before sin, Adam and Eve weren't self-conscious about being naked because they were focused on loving God and each other, not on themselves. They were without shame because they had no *reason* for shame, no barriers in their relationship with God or each other.

But what was the very first thing Adam and Eve did after they sinned? They tried to cover their nakedness and hide from God. They felt ashamed.

Protection from the danger of use

Sin distorted the proper focus of sex from expressing spousal love to experiencing physical pleasure. Now Adam and Eve knew that it was possible to use and be used. Now they had a valid reason to keep their guard up. A barrier arose in their relationship.

Think about a time when you met a new group of people. Maybe you hesitated to reveal too much about yourself right away. You hesitated in order to protect yourself against being rejected or used.

Before sin, Adam and Eve could be naked without shame because they had nothing to hide *from*. In our sin-stricken world, though, it's different. The shame we feel when our bodies are exposed reveals the sad, dangerous reality of *use*—using others and being used by them. Concupiscence, which makes us lean toward sin, tempts us to misuse other people as objects for personal satisfaction—or even misuse our own bodies as tools to manipulate others or gain attention.

It is no longer prudent to be naked without shame. We wear clothes to protect us not only from the weather but also from the dangers of being used. Our bodies are sacred and should be protected from anyone who would treat us like objects instead of persons with great dignity.

But there is great news! Jesus redeems and heals everything. Instead of following our fallen nature into regret and anxiety, we can follow Jesus into freedom and peace.

Beauty and power

God designed the sexual act as a gift for spouses to show their love, bond intimately with each other, and bring new human persons into existence. Giving yourself to another person through sex is an act of emotional, physical, and spiritual vulnerability. Sex can nurture beautiful intimacy when it's connected to God's design. When sex is *disconnected* from God's design, we suffer.

Who can you give yourself to without fear or insecurity? Who can you trust to love you and not use you? Who can you be sure is faithful to you? Is it someone you're trying to impress or hardly know? Someone who might dump you in a few months? Someone who may not even be in your life in a few years?

You can give a total gift of yourself only to someone who will give a total self-gift to you. Where does this kind of commitment exist? Dating relationships have a certain level of commitment that can grow over time—but a

Time, history, and progress don't change our human nature, God's design, or what brings us true joy.

dating couple is not yet fully free and faithful to each other. When are two people vowed to each other this way? In marriage! We should save sex for marriage because the language of the body, communicated through sex, tells the truth only in marriage.

You might be thinking, Isn't this just some old-fashioned rule that nobody really follows anymore?

Time, history, and progress don't change our human nature, God's design, or what brings us true joy. Sex means the same thing now that it did when God first invented it. Sometimes the world or our desires tempt us to believe that sex isn't a big deal or that we don't need boundaries with sexual expression. But sex *is* a big deal. Sex connects people and brings forth new life.

God doesn't want us to pretend that we do not experience sexual attraction and desire. He doesn't want us to repress our affection for those we love. He doesn't want us to just forget the whole subject until adulthood. What he does want is for us to experience the full goodness of his design, not just bits of pleasure.

So what are you supposed to do about attraction and desire in relationships if you are still years away from marriage?

Chastity empowers

Chastity is a yes to living and loving through the gift of our sexuality as God intended. It empowers us to love ourselves and others rightly through the language of our bodies. Chastity means living our sexuality in the way that tells the truth about our identity, vocation, and relationships. We grow

in the virtue of chastity by learning self-control, modesty, and respect for ourselves and others.

Chastity brings happiness and peace to our relationships. It allows us to love and to know if we are being loved.

Like all virtues, chastity is for everyone: single people, priests, religious brothers and sisters, and married couples. Of course, we live it out in different ways depending on our vocation.

In marriage, sex expresses what is really true in that relationship: free, total, faithful commitment that is fruitful (which means open to life). Spouses practice chastity when they express their vows through sex.

When people are single, dating, or engaged, practicing chastity includes abstinence. **Abstinence** is refraining from intimate sexual activity outside of marriage. Because the relationship has not yet become fully free, total, faithful, and fruitful, sexual activity outside of marriage does *not* express the truth. Only in marriage can this language of the body be truthful. Only in marriage can the body truly say, "I give myself completely to you. I am ready to spend the rest of my life with you, and have a family with you, and stay faithful to you in good times and in bad." Any activity that may cause us or another person to become sexually aroused—things like passionate and prolonged kissing—should be saved for marriage. Why? Through the language of our bodies, these activities say that we are ready for more sexual contact. When we are not married, we are *not* ready for sexual contact, so this is not a truthful expression.

But chastity goes much deeper. Chastity also means maintaining interior purity. This means striving to keep not only our actions but also our thoughts, imaginations, and hearts free from lust. The vice of **lust** is the opposite of chastity. Lust sees people as objects to be used rather than persons to be loved. Lust distorts sex into an expression of selfishness instead of self-gift. Lust doesn't hurt only others; it also deeply damages our understanding of our true identity.

You are not an object. You are worthy of being loved.

St. John Paul II emphasized that using another person is the opposite of love. Chastity helps us develop the habit of loving others rather than using them. Practicing chastity inwardly (in our minds and hearts) and outwardly (by our actions) trains us to see each other as we ought. Chastity says yes to love. Saying yes to the right action at the right time means saying no to the wrong action at the wrong time. It's not easy, but it is worth the effort because it leads us to what we really want.

Modesty

Modesty is another virtue that flows from chastity. **Modesty** is choosing clothes that express the truth: our goodness and beauty don't come from how we look on the outside or how much attention we get for our appearance. Our goodness and beauty stem from being loved by God and being true to the way he made us to be.

Clothes should let us be free to be our authentic selves, not make us feel like we have to show off our bodies to get people to like us or give us attention. Immodest clothes encourage us to see others as a collection of body parts rather than as a whole person.

Along with clothing, we can also practice modesty in our speech, entertainment choices, and jokes.

Both chastity and modesty free us from shame and insecurity. Both make us free, equipped, capable, strong, open, more available to hear God, and more able to love others unselfishly. When we are free to be ourselves, we are free to tell the truth with our bodies and speak love with our bodies. We are free to become the men and women God made us to be.

> "Modesty protects the mystery of persons and their love. It encourages patience and moderation in loving relationships. ... It inspires one's choice of clothing. It keeps silence or reserve where there is evident risk of unhealthy curiosity. It is discreet."—*CCC 2522*

IF YOU ASK ME ...

- _____ *is a good role model of modesty.*

Protecting your goal

Whether it's volleyball, lacrosse, football, softball, basketball, baseball, or soccer, a good team needs both an offense and a defense. Both are critical in practicing chastity, too. The offense is pursuing your goal: the freedom to love rightly, both now and in your future vocation. The defense is protecting that goal: right now, this means abstinence. But defense is not about sitting around passively, doing nothing. You're doing something active with a specific purpose.

Like all virtues, chastity requires practice. As with modesty, we develop chastity in our jokes, speech, the movies we watch, the music we listen to, and the online places we go. Telling dirty jokes, listening to sexually explicit music, or looking at porn disrespects and distorts our sexuality from self-gift into self-satisfaction. Guarding these habits helps us guard the purity of our minds and hearts.

Let's be honest: none of this is easy. Sexual attraction and desire are natural and good, but they can turn into temptation, even sin, if we allow ourselves to get carried away. Be honest with God when you are tempted to be selfish in some way. You might say, "Lord, I'm really attracted to this person. Thank you for making someone so amazing. But I know you made me to give, not to take. Give me the grace to treat this person with respect at all times."

Training for love

Relationships between the two sexes are meant to train us for healthy marriages in the future. Yet we see a lot of problematic training. Many people view dating as a game. Many people mock chastity. Training wrongly now doesn't lead to loving rightly later.

If you want more than the insecurity, drama, cheating, abuse, breakups, divorce, confusion, and the pain of lust, choose the freedom and love of chastity. If you want fulfilling relationships now and a successful future marriage, train rightly. Here are habits you can focus on:

- Treat others, especially those you date, the way you would want your future spouse, your brother or sister, or even your own children to be treated. You wouldn't want them to be used as objects. Set the same standard for yourself.

- Choose wisely what you listen to, watch, and read.

- Use respectful language.

- Spend your time on things that build up you and others.

- Find solid Catholic role models to talk with about your personal journey.

- Work on friendships with others who have the same goals.

Remember: you are created by God for the triumph of love.

IF YOU ASK ME ...

- *A couple I know who have a happy, healthy marriage are _____. I can tell because* _____.

- *One thing I can work on to practice chastity and love is* _____.

Quick Quiz

1. Sex is first about our _____ as men and women created in God's
    _____ and_____.

2. The unique, different characteristics of _____ and _____
    bring out the best in the other. This difference is called _____.

3. Sexual intimacy is true to God's design when it is free, total, faithful, and fruitful (open to
    new life). This can happen only within _____.

4. A husband and wife's faithful love for each other reflects the love of the _____:
    the Father, the Son, and the Holy Spirit.

5. _____ is the urge to cover up or hide something from God, others, or ourselves.

6. Chastity means living our _____ in the way that tells the truth about
    our identity, vocation, and relationships.

7. Lust sees people as _____ to be used.

8. Modest clothing helps protect us and others from being treated like a collection of
    _____.

9. To have fulfilling relationships now and a successful marriage later, we should train for
    authentic love by practicing _____.

 Video 3: Witness and Wrap-Up

Top Ten Dos and Don'ts

After reflecting on the virtues of chastity and modesty, create a "top ten" list of dos and don'ts for people your age. What habits are important for living out a life of chastity and modesty? Remember that chastity and modesty are not limited to sexual actions; they also affect our speech, imagination, entertainment choices, jokes, clothing, and more. Use the space below to create your list as a personal journal entry or with a partner or small group.

1. _____

2. _____

3. _____

4. _____

5. _____

6. _____

7. _____

8. _____

9. _____

10. _____

Got It?

Chastity is not a no.

Chastity is yes!

To really love,

To never use,

And to bring out the best.

CLOSING PRAYER

+ In the name of the Father, and of the Son, and of the Holy Spirit. Amen.

In the divine image, Lord, you created him; male and female you created them. O Lord, you made me as a gift for others and gave me attractions in order to build relationships of love. Help me accept myself daily as a gift and pursue the gift of the other sex with purity of mind, heart, and body.

Jesus, your Mother Mary helps us to be pure in all things, so we turn to her now as we pray, *Hail Mary* ... Amen.

VOCABULARY

sex: Sex is first about our identity as male or female created in God's image and likeness. Sex also refers to acts of physical intimacy between a husband and wife, especially intercourse. Sex expresses spouses' invisible gift of self and union with each other through the visible gift and union of their bodies. As marriage is a free, total, faithful, and fruitful union, sex is a free, total, faithful bodily union that has the potential fruitfulness of new life.

spousal: Relating to or shared between a husband and a wife.

"Male and female he created them": This phrase from Genesis 1 reveals that from the beginning, God designed sex to communicate the love between a husband and wife in the relationship of marriage.

chastity: A virtue that empowers us to love ourselves and others rightly through the language of our bodies. Chastity means living our sexuality in the way that tells the truth about our identity, vocation, and relationships throughout our lives; it also means striving for purity of mind, heart, and body. Chastity is a virtue for everyone in all vocations.

abstinence: Refraining from something, such as abstaining from meat on Fridays in Lent. In relationships, abstinence is refraining from intimate sexual activity outside of marriage. Abstinence is a necessary part of chastity for unmarried people, but abstinence by itself is not the same as chastity.

lust: A vice that sees people as objects to be used rather than persons to be loved. Lust distorts sex into an expression of selfishness instead of self-gift. Lust damages our understanding of our true identity.

modesty: A virtue that empowers us to respect the dignity of our bodies and God's design for sexuality in how we dress, speak, and act. Modesty expresses the reality that our goodness and beauty don't come from getting attention with our appearance or outward behavior but from being loved by God and from being ourselves the way he made us to be.

complementarity: The unique, different characteristics of maleness and femaleness created by God as a gift to bring out the best in each other and call us to communion and self-gift.

shame: The experience of Adam and Eve after the Fall, and all of us since then, fearing others as a threat to our dignity. At the same time, shame reminds us to recognize and protect our value.

Lesson Six: What Is Love?

LOVE VERSUS USE

OPENING PRAYER

+ In the name of the Father, and of the Son, and of the Holy Spirit. Amen.

In the divine image, Lord, you created him; male and female you created them. God our Father, you made us male and female, created in your image and likeness. Help us grow into the men and women that you created us to be. Show us the goodness of our bodies and the right way to honor the brothers and sisters around us as a constant reminder of their dignity.

Jesus, you taught us to address your Father as you did, and so, in the Holy Spirit, we pray, *Our Father* ... Amen.

"A person's rightful due is to be treated as **an object of love**, not as an object for use."

—St. John Paul II, Love and Responsibility

THE BIG PICTURE

How many songs, movies, poems, plays, artworks, and books throughout history are about love? Love fills our human experience! It occupies our minds and hearts; it keeps us up at night; it motivates us, breaks us, puts us back together again; it shapes our lives. Love can also seem confusing, but we can't escape our longing for love. Love answers those big questions—*Who am I?* and *Where am I going?*—because we are made by love, for love.

So, what is love? A feeling? A force? A chemical reaction? If we tune in, we can hear in our hearts an echo of the original, beautiful story of love that began in the Garden of Eden. It's a story of striving, sacrificing, and self-gift. It's a story about why we exist and what life is for. In the story of love, our hearts can be untangled and our desires can be untwisted. The story of love is *your* story. It begins when you dare to ask the simplest but most important question: What is love?

STORY STARTER

As their conversation came to an end, his heart started beating faster. He was going to say it. They had been dating for several weeks. He thought about her constantly. He messaged her every morning when he woke up and referred to her as his girlfriend. It was time.

He had never said the big three words to a girl before, but he knew that some of his friends had. He wanted this to be a real relationship. All afternoon he had been imagining this moment and mentally practicing.

"My mom says I have to go to bed," she said.

"Oh, okay," he said. "Yeah, I should go to bed, too." He felt a lump forming in his throat. His heart bounced like a basketball in his chest.

"See you at school," she said.

"Okay, yeah. And ... I love you," he blurted out, ten times more quickly than he meant to. Did his voice really sound like that? He felt all the blood rush to his face. Suddenly, he felt exposed.

Silence. "Hello?" he asked.

"Um ... we're in seventh grade," she responded awkwardly.

He wasn't sure exactly what he had expected, but this definitely was not the response he had hoped for.

She continued, "Do you even know what love is?"

He hadn't really thought about that, but he said anyway, "Of course I do."

She didn't say anything right away. "I really like you, but ... I'm not sure about saying that yet."

The dose of reality, hard as it was to hear, made sense. "Okay," he managed. "Good night."

"Good night. See you at school," she said.

Later, as he tried to fall asleep, that big question raced through his mind. *What is love?* He realized that he had no idea. Was it a feeling? His feelings had to be *something*. Was love a place people "fall into"? If he wasn't there yet, why did he feel this way?

He eventually drifted to sleep without any answers.

IF YOU ASK ME ...

- *When I think about love, _____ is a song that comes to mind.*

- *I think _____ (movie, book, or show) is a good love story.*

- *_____ is someone in my life who shows me what real love is.*

- *My definition of love so far is _____.*

Video 1: Introduction

IF YOU ASK ME ...

- *What do you think love is?* _____

_____

_____

Video 2: To the Core

VIDEO QUESTIONS

1. **True or False:** Love goes much deeper than feelings.

2. **True or False:** Jim's gift to Aimee was important because it was expensive.

3. **True or False:** The opposite of love is use.

What is love?

Ask ten people this question, and you will get ten different answers. We all want love, but it's hard to define. Just think of all the ways we use the word "love." We *love* ice cream and *love* our families—but these obviously are not the same thing.

In fact, love is the difference between how you respond to things and to people. Your "love" for ice cream is based totally on what you get from it— the great taste, the creamy sweetness, the cool-down on a hot day. Ice cream is an object you use for your personal pleasure.

Love for people, however, isn't based on what you get from them. Love sees that a person's worth doesn't depend on what he or she can offer. People are precious simply because they exist. Love says, "I am so glad that *you*

exist. The world is so much better with you in it." Love wants the best for another person. Love and **use** are total opposites.

Think of God's love. Does God value people because of their beauty or popularity? Does God take advantage of people? Of course not. God loves you just because he does. He loves you without any conditions. In fact, you wouldn't even exist if God didn't love you into existence.

God made things to be used and people to be loved, but too often we get it backward. Do you know anyone who is "friends" with someone just to be popular? Has anyone been nice to you just so you would do them a favor? Treating others as objects to control, manipulate, and use is never satisfying and always destructive.

Concupiscence means we are always going to struggle with selfishness, but as a relationship gets deeper, love should grow deeper, too, and become more and more like God's sacrificial, unconditional love.

You need to know how love looks and acts so your relationships can become a mature participation in God's love, not the selfishness of use.

Love in balance: *eros* and *agape*

Imagine this scenario: Daniel and Mia have been dating for a few months. He really cares about her. One night Mia announces, "Hey, great news! My parents finally agreed to pay for me to go to summer camp with my best friends." It really is great news; Mia has hoped all year that summer camp would work out. However, camp means that Daniel won't see her for a few weeks. So he has a

choice. He can sacrifice his own disappointment and be happy because he wants Mia to have a good experience—or he can complain and make her feel guilty for causing him to miss her for a few weeks. Which response is real love? (If you said real love was Daniel's joyful sacrifice on Mia's behalf, you'd be right.)

We naturally want to be close to those we love. The desire for closeness is called **eros**. In romantic relationships, especially in the beginning, the desire to be together can dominate. You might think about him or her all the time. You might want to share every little thought and moment. While it's never healthy to obsess or isolate yourself from other friendships, the desire to be together is good, normal, and a sign of maturing.

Yet the higher part of love goes beyond just wanting to be together. It's about wanting what is truly best for the other person. This is called **agape**. *Agape* inspires us to make sacrifices to achieve the other person's good. Maybe you let your friends pick the movie or go ahead of you in line. Why? You want good things for them.

Agape is also present in true romantic love. Maybe you have seen husbands and wives make sacrifices so their spouses' lives can be easier, better, or happier. This is another way marriage is an important teacher and witness beyond the spouses themselves. Seeing spouses live out *agape* inspires us to strive for self-giving, sacrificial love, too.

But what happens if there is *eros* without *agape*—attraction and desire without empathy and sacrifice*?*

Left on its own, *eros* becomes jealous and possessive. *Eros* without *agape* becomes focused on personal satisfaction. It leads to insecurity, anxiety, and manipulation. Eventually, the relationship isn't about love at all—just self-centeredness. If you want to be with someone more than you want what is best for him or her, a relationship can break.

But in a relationship where *eros* and *agape* are properly balanced, there is attraction *with* empathy, a desire for closeness *with* a willingness to sacrifice for the other. This genuine love is a true self-gift that says "you" more than "me." As a fan spreads cool air outward on a hot summer day, a balanced relationship refreshes everybody around it. An imbalanced relationship, however, is like a giant vacuum that pulls everything inward and doesn't give anything back.

Maybe you have seen this kind of relationship, where selfishness dominates. The couple makes others uncomfortable because they are so clingy. They go too far too fast. They are jealous and possessive. They constantly message and obsess about each other. They may fall into endless drama, fighting, or a cycle of breaking up and getting back together. These are signs of an immature relationship that is not about the other person's happiness. The relationship is not a gift but an exhausting, confusing chore.

Agape protects *eros* from becoming selfish. The virtue of chastity empowers us to choose *agape*, even if it means less physical contact than we might desire. God knows it isn't easy, and he wants us to share our struggles with him. When we call on him, he will always help us grow in inner strength, purity of heart, and real love.

IF YOU ASK ME ...

Listen to a popular love song and determine whether it describes properly balanced, "real-deal" love or if it describes unbalanced love full of lust and possessiveness.

Song: _____

Artist: _____

Number of times the lyrics say "I" or "me": _____

Number of times the lyrics say "you": _____

Number of times the lyrics say "we": _____

Which of the following statements best describes the song?

    "This is a total no-brainer; this song is lustful and just plain vulgar."

    "The lyrics seem romantic at first, but they are really about using someone."

    "This song is ridiculously possessive; the artist sounds jealous."

    "The lyrics sound sweet, but if you listen closely, they are kind of self-centered."

    "The lyrics express genuine love; it might be great for the first dance at a wedding."

Think about your life. How clearly does your world show real love?

Think about the music you listen to, what you watch, where you go online, or the stuff you post and talk about.

Think about how dating looks. Think about the way people talk about relationships, sex, and love. Are you seeing the desire to be close (*eros*) in balance with a willingness to sacrifice for the other person (*agape*)? Are you seeing sex described as a sacred union of self-gift between spouses? Are you seeing chastity embraced as a virtue that gives us freedom?

Good news: God gave us the Ten Commandments to guide us through whatever confusion the world tries to serve us. These commandments offer us clear instructions for happiness. The boundaries set by the commandments protect us from the consequences of using and being used, show us what actions make us happy, and help us understand what actions ensure truthful language of our bodies.

The world has changed dramatically since the commandments were first given to Moses. We deal with questions and issues that didn't exist twenty years ago, much less several thousand. But even as technology develops, human nature does not change.

One reason Jesus established his Catholic Church is to apply the commandments to modern issues. The Church teaches us what actions are violations of the commandments (sins) that cut us off from love. The Sixth and Ninth Commandments especially focus on sexual issues.

> **Sixth Commandment:** You shall not commit adultery.
>
> **Ninth Commandment:** You shall not covet your neighbor's wife.
>
> These two commandments teach us to respect marriage as a sacred bond and to see others as persons to love, not objects for use.

Here are major ways that these commandments apply to our world today.

What's wrong with pornography?

Pornography includes images, videos, or written material intended to arouse lust. Porn is deeply destructive. It harms the people involved by using them as objects for pleasure. Porn shows intimate body parts but fails to show full human *persons* who have dignity because they are created by God in his image. Because it mocks, distorts, and hides human dignity, porn is gravely immoral. Using porn can also be gravely sinful.

Porn damages our ability to have truly loving relationships in *real* life. How? It trains us to use people, which is the opposite of love. It trains us to see another person as a product for sale or a collection of body parts we can use for our own pleasure instead of someone worthy of respect. Porn transforms sex from self-gift into total selfishness.

Porn has other long-term dangers. Research has shown that repeatedly using porn changes a person's brain.* Lust becomes a vice (a strong, destructive habit) that can be extremely difficult to break. Using porn damages your long-term ability to bond with the opposite sex. This harm also comes from shows, movies, books, and music that are intended to arouse lust.

There is help available to overcome this vice, even if someone feels trapped in a cycle of using porn for a long time. You can do the following if someone you know is using porn:

- Let your friend know you are worried about the harm porn can cause.

- Encourage your friend to talk to a parent or another trusted adult.

- Most important, remind your friend that healing begins with Jesus forgiving our sins in the Sacrament of Reconciliation.

---

* Fight the New Drug, "How Porn Can Change the Brain," May 11, 2021, fightthenewdrug.org.

How should we use devices?

Sadly, sharing sexual images, words, jokes, and messages on devices is not uncommon. Many people mistakenly think, *If so many people do it, it can't be that bad. This doesn't really mean anything anyway.*

First, every single thing you share digitally exists for your whole life and even beyond. Once you click "send," "share," or "post," your images and words never disappear. Everything you share can be forwarded or posted somewhere you didn't intend. Sexual images, words, jokes, and messages can be discovered by your siblings, parents, classmates, and teachers. The risk extends years into your future, when college administrators or employers find your content.

Never share or post anything immodest, lustful, harmful, false, or objectifying. Whenever you let someone take a photo of you, be sure you are dressed modestly.

But even worse are the consequences experienced in your emotions and relationships. We often say and do things online that we would hold off from doing in real life. It's not because we are more truly "free" online; it's because the digital space makes us feel more removed from the consequences. In real life, holding back saves us and others a lot of hurt and insecurity. The digital world can seem like it's not quite "real"—but a real, personal exchange does take place. Digitally presenting yourself as an object or viewing others as objects causes lasting, real-life damage.

God did not make you or any other person to be an object. The only proper response to a human person is love. Sharing videos or photos mocks the sacredness of the body and harms our ability to experience real love, and it damages others in the same way. Good choices protect you and others, both now and later in life.

Why save sex for marriage?

The sixth commandment teaches us that sex is for marriage. The sins of adultery and fornication both violate the free, total, faithful, and fruitful nature of sex. **Adultery** is sex between a married person and someone who is not his or her spouse. Many people call this "cheating." **Fornication** is sex between unmarried people.

> "Fornication ... is gravely contrary to the dignity of persons and of human sexuality which is naturally ordered to the good of spouses and the generation ... of children."—CCC 2353

For a couple to have a joyful, lifelong marriage, they need to be committed and willing to make sacrifices for each other. You don't develop these virtues just by exchanging vows. You must practice them *before* marriage. Sex outside of marriage is practicing the opposite. It places personal desire over commitment to God's plan for you and the other person. Your commitment and willingness to sacrifice for your future spouse begin now. If you can't say no to sex before marriage, something is lacking in the requirements of real love.

Sometimes people ask, "But what if we really do love each other now? How could sex be wrong if it's connected to love?"

If we really love someone, we want the highest good for him or her—not something less—and we definitely do not want something harmful. Sex is meant to express love that wants the highest good. It is also an act of vulnerability and openness to new life, so sex is always a big deal. When is that vulnerability truly best? When is opening up the possibility of becoming parents truly best? Only in the free, total, faithful, fruitful relationship of marriage.

Saving sexual activity for marriage says "I love you" with the language of the body. "I love you so much that I want what is best for you more than I want what feels good right now. I love you so much that I am *not* willing to expose you to sin, anxiety, hardship, insecurity, pain, or anything less than the best." Again, chastity empowers us to make these truly loving choices. Don't you want the person you really love to have the most freedom now and the best future possible?

> "I love you so much that I want what is best for you more than I want what feels good right now."

How far is too far when you're dating?

Consider this: What is dating for? While dating is exciting and fun, the true purpose of dating is to find a spouse. At this point in your life, are you really ready to focus on that? You may even have more fun and be more relaxed if you concentrate on friendships and group activities rather than exclusive dating.

If you do start dating sometime in the future, how do you show that you care about and really like someone? Remember that God's boundaries are not just rules but instructions for true happiness. You can trust that when God gives us a boundary, it marks the best path for everyone involved.

While you won't find a Bible verse that says, "Thou shall not kiss for more than ten seconds," you can judge what behaviors are too far if they cross these boundaries:

- You are thinking about how far you can get with someone else.

- You are making people around you uncomfortable.

- Your behavior tempts someone else to lust or commit another sin. Jesus gave extremely serious warnings about the evil of leading others into sin.

- Your behavior is focused on experiencing pleasure, not expressing love and affection.

- Your body is becoming aroused (starting to feel sexual pleasure).

- The language of your body or someone else's becomes sexual.

- You are touching private body parts on someone else or letting someone touch yours.

- The language of your body or someone else's says, "I am married to you."

Sex always says, "I freely give myself totally to you, and only you, forever—and I am open to having a baby with you." Such a dramatic statement cannot be made truthfully outside of marriage, because marriage is the only relationship of a free, total, faithful, and fruitful self-gift between two people.

These boundaries do not exist because sex is bad in any way. God created sex, and he creates only good, true, and beautiful things. But you don't have to settle for the insecurity and anxiety that come with the world's immature understanding of sex. You can have more: the true beauty and goodness of God's plan, and nothing less.

What if I have failed (once or many times) in chastity?

We all sin, even if we know better. Even if we want better, sometimes we fail anyway because we are all weak. When we sin, we should run back to Jesus, who wants to heal us and help us. If you have failed to live up to chastity in some way, don't give up. Sin is a lie, and Satan often whispers other lies to us after we sin: *You can't change. Things are hopeless. If you can't be perfect, it's pointless to try.*

Sin harms us, and we should take it seriously. But even sin cannot take away our ability to repent and recommit to real love. When we repent, God can restore what we need for a future full of hope. God is the one who loves you most. Never be afraid to go to him for mercy, which he will always give. Never be afraid to ask him for help again—because he will always say yes.

Go to Confession. Remember that Satan tempts us to hide our sins, but God wants to free us from

When we confess our sins, God gives us grace and strength to grow in purity and freedom.

them. When we confess our sins, God gives us grace and strength to grow in purity and freedom. Even if we fail and must go to Confession often, every Act of Contrition is a new commitment to chastity. Pray for grace to choose love instead of selfishness. Share your struggles with your parents or trusted advisors. Go to Mass every Sunday and receive Jesus in the Eucharist. The closer you are to him, the closer you will be to your goal of real love, both now and in the future. Empowered by chastity, you can say to your future spouse, "I loved you before I even knew you." Who wouldn't want that kind of love?

Quick Quiz

1. God made _____ to be used and _____ to be loved.

2. The opposite of real love is _____.

3. The part of love that wants what is best for the other person is called _____.

4. The part of love also that wants to be close to the person you are attracted to is called _____.

5. The desire for physical closeness needs to be balanced and protected from becoming _____.

6. The Ten Commandments give us clear_____ for _____.

7. Pornography trains us to _____ people, the opposite of love.

8. A joyful, lifelong marriage requires practicing commitment and sacrifice _____ marriage.

 Video 3: Witness and Wrap-Up

Chastity Myths

Below are some myths about chastity and sex. Together with a partner or small group, identify which you think are the top three chastity myths in our culture and say why they are not true. Then write a sentence or two explaining the truth.

1. If my boyfriend or girlfriend is sexually tempted, that's his or her problem, not mine.

   _____

2. Sex is not a big deal—it's just something fun to do.

   _____

3. Having sex will improve my dating relationship.

   _____

4. Having sex will make me more mature.

   _____

5. Sexual content in entertainment doesn't affect me.

   _____

6. If you make a sexual mistake, you can't go back to chastity.

   _____

7. Chastity is just about not having sex.

   _____

8. Chastity ends at marriage.

   _____

9. Chastity is about saying no.

   _____

10. Chastity is impossible to live out in today's oversexualized world.

    _____

Got It?

Love people. Use things. (Not the other way around.)

CLOSING PRAYER

+ In the name of the Father, and of the Son, and of the Holy Spirit. Amen.

In the divine image, Lord, you created him; male and female you created them. God our Father, you are love, and you have made us for love. Thank you for the people in our lives who have shown us what love really is and how love really acts. Open our eyes to the ways we can love like you today.

Jesus, your Mother Mary teaches us to love generously, so
we turn to her now as we pray, *Hail Mary* ... Amen.

VOCABULARY

agape: The form of love that genuinely wants what is good for the other and works to achieve it. *Agape* isn't focused on self and gives without expecting anything in return. *Agape* inspires us to make sacrifices for those we love.

eros: The form of love that wants to be close to the person you love. *Eros* must always be balanced with *agape* to protect it from selfishness or possessiveness.

use: This is the opposite of love because it treats a person like an object for some pleasure or gain instead of respecting his or her dignity.

adultery: The sin of sexual activity between a married person and someone who is not his or her spouse.

fornication: The sin of sexual activity between people who are not married.

pornography: Anything that includes images, videos, or written material intended to arouse lust.

Lesson Seven: Vocation to Holiness

GOD'S CALL, MY RESPONSE

OPENING PRAYER

+ In the name of the Father, and of the Son, and of the Holy Spirit. Amen.

In the divine image, Lord, you created him; male and female you created them. You made each of us unique and unrepeatable so we can shine light in a dark world. Give us the grace to listen to your voice. Set our hearts on fire for the great adventure of saying yes to you and yes to holiness.

Jesus, your heart burned with love and beat in perfect obedience to the Father, and so, in the Holy Spirit, we pray for the same love and fidelity, *Our Father ...* Amen.

"In the hidden recesses of the human heart the grace of a vocation takes the form of a dialogue. It is a dialogue between Christ and an individual, in which a personal invitation is given. Christ calls the person by name and says: 'Come, follow me.' This call, this mysterious inner voice of Christ, is heard most clearly in silence and prayer. Its acceptance is an act of faith."

—St. John Paul II, Homily, India, 1986

THE BIG PICTURE

When was the last time you just sat in silence without music or videos or scrolling a screen? The world overloads our senses. There is an endless loop of things to watch, listen to, and look at. Flashy ads and pinging notifications constantly try to pull us deeper into devices. We are rarely just still and quiet.

God's voice is constant, too. But God isn't pushy or demanding or flashy. He calls us with a steady voice of peace. When we turn off the distractions and noise and truly listen, we can hear God calling each of us to holiness.

Maybe you've always thought of holiness as something for a few special people, or maybe only for people in certain vocations, or maybe for people who are much older. The truth is that holiness is for everyone, everywhere, at every age—for you, right here, right now. Holiness is the adventure of becoming who God created us to be. Holiness isn't boring or predictable. Holiness doesn't change us into someone we're not. God made each of us unique and unrepeatable, and he wants our differences to shine, not be covered up. When we say yes to following Jesus, holiness shines like light in the darkness.

In the future, holiness may include answering the call to a vocation like marriage, the priesthood, or religious life. But holiness starts today as you follow Jesus at home, at school, on the sports field, on the stage, in your hobbies, in the way you interact with technology, and more.

You're headed toward a future of love in your relationships and ultimately in heaven. Holiness is how you're going to get there.

STORY STARTER

I know it's a cliché, and people always say it—but the day Aimee and I got married really was the best day of my life. When my best man, Greg, woke me up that morning, I jumped up, excited to put on my tuxedo. With my red hair and scruffy beard, I looked like a cross between James Bond and the Lucky Charms leprechaun.

I had way too much nervous energy just to hang out at the hotel. I asked Greg to drive me to the Eucharistic Adoration chapel where I had proposed to Aimee months before. There I knelt down, had a heart-to-heart with Jesus, and tried to prepare for the big moment.

We left the chapel and headed to the church, with an hour left until the wedding began. Every minute seemed like ten. I paced. I prayed. I waited … and waited … and waited. Finally, guests started arriving. I headed to my position by the altar rail and watched as people filled the church. Before I knew it, I was standing next to Greg as music played and bridesmaids came down the aisle.

Then—a burst of light! The heavy church door opened. It was better than a vision in any movie when I finally saw my beautiful bride enter on her father's arm. With every step they took down the aisle, my heart beat faster until at last she was only two feet away.

Her father reached out to shake my hand, but then he stopped. Instead of the traditional short handshake, he pressed something cool and metallic into my palm. "There was once a husband who loved his bride so much that he would do anything for her," Aimee's dad said. "Anything."

I knew his words were intense and serious, but they didn't really register at first. When he let go of my hand, I looked down to see the object he had placed there.

It was a small silver crucifix. Suddenly I understood. The husband was Jesus; the bride was the Church. Jesus had done not only anything, but everything, for his bride. He gave his life in love. This was the same reason I stood at the altar that day: to give my life in love for my bride.

To be like Christ to the person I love the most was—and still is—an awesome call to holiness.— *Colin MacIver*

IF YOU ASK ME ...

- *What do you think is the best sign of holiness? (Circle one.)*
    - » Kindness
    - » Joyfulness
    - » Honesty
    - » Obedience
    - » Humility
    - » Chastity
    - » Piety (going to church, wearing a cross, etc.)
- *I think that (single life, married life, religious life, ordained life) is the holiest because*
_____ .

- *A girl around my age who is holy is _____ because she _____ .*

- *A boy around my age who is holy is _____ because he _____ .*

Video 1: Introduction

IF YOU ASK ME ...

- *What do you think the voice of God sounds like? How do you listen for God's voice?*

_____

_____

Video 2: To the Core

VIDEO QUESTIONS

1. **True or False:** Everyone is called to holiness

2. **True or False:** Being holy means being perfect.

3. **True or False:** Future relationships don't need to look like the brokenness we see or may have come from.

Vocation to holiness

Who should be holy? Most of us think of priests and nuns. But what about your parents or other married people? What about your friends? What about *you*?

Jesus said "Follow me" to all kinds of people, in all kinds of situations. He called all of them to holiness. But what does holiness really mean?

Holiness isn't wearing a giant cross or preaching on the sidewalks. Holiness means "reserved for" or "dedicated." Who should be reserved for and dedicated to God? Everyone. *You!*

God is calling you to holiness through a particular **vocation**, a path in life that will best fulfill your strengths, heal your weaknesses, and help you become a saint. Your vocation may be marriage, the priesthood, or religious life. Every vocation is a calling to holiness. Through your vocation, God will prepare you ultimately to be with him in heaven.

Even if you feel unsure about your vocation in the future, your call to holiness starts today. "God stuff" isn't for when you're older. You are called to be holy *now*—as a student, a friend, and a son or daughter in your family. Just as Jesus called St. Peter and St. Mary Magdalene, he's calling you: "Follow me."

> "Holiness is not the luxury of the few, but a simple duty for you and for me."—*St. Teresa of Calcutta*

IF YOU ASK ME ...

- *Something that helps people grow in holiness is* _____.

- *Something that prevents people from growing in holiness* _____.

Saint You

In this program, you have done some pretty intense thinking about who you are, where you're going, and how to get there. These questions lead you toward fulfilling your call to holiness and becoming the saint God made you to be.

Maybe the thought of being a saint sounds overwhelming. Does sainthood mean losing your identity or living a boring life? The truth is that the closer you get to God, the more you become your true self. Holiness is the full realization of your unique personality. In sainthood, your individuality reaches perfection. God wants you to be inspired by St. Teresa of Calcutta, St. Paul Miki, St. Josephine Bakhita, St. Kateri Tekakwitha, and St. John Paul II—but he doesn't want you to be copies of them. God wants you to become "Saint [insert your name here]."

The lives of the saints reveal how diverse holiness is. St. John Bosco and St. Teresa of Ávila were practical jokers. Ven. Augustus Tolton escaped from slavery and became the first black American priest. St. Joan of Arc led the French army to victory in battle when she was just a teenager.

Bl. Miguel Pro wore disguises to escape from his enemies. St. Thérèse of Lisieux loved to perform plays. St. Pio of Pietrelcina bilocated and could read souls. St. Gianna Molla was both a mom and a doctor. St. Maximilian Kolbe ran a radio show. Bl. Columba Kang Wan-suk helped hide priests during a persecution. St. Margaret was shipwrecked and became a queen. Bl. Carlo Acutis built websites. St. Jacinta Marto saw an apparition of Our Lady. Do these sound like boring lives?

It is sin, not holiness, that dulls our individuality. As St. Catherine of Siena reminds us, if we are what we ought to be, we will set the world on fire.

Your vocation includes God's call to a particular way of life within the Church. God may call you to be a married person, nun, sister, consecrated single person, monk, religious brother, deacon, or priest. All these paths reflect Jesus' love for the Church and require self-gift. Wherever God calls you, there you will find the most joy and freedom to be yourself along with the best path to sainthood.

Called to marriage

The most common vocation is **marriage.** Marriage means much more than a legal contract or sharing a household. Marriage is an exclusive relationship of committed love between one man and one woman until death. St. Paul calls marriage "a great mystery" (Ephesians 5:32). A husband and wife are called to be a visible reminder of the love that Jesus has for his Bride, the Church, which is revealed especially in his Passion and Resurrection.

The marriage vows exchanged between a man and a woman are a great sign of God's love in four major ways:

- The couple makes their vows freely, reminding us that God's love is given freely.

- The couple vows to give themselves totally to each other.

- The couple vows faithfulness until death, reminding us of God's eternally faithful love.

- The couple also vows to accept any children that God sends as a gift. As spousal love overflows into a family, it reminds us of God's *life-giving* love and of how precious each human person is to God.

Much more than the dress, cake, and rings, the wedding vows are the most important part of marriage. The whole purpose of marriage is your free, total, faithful, fruitful commitment to your

spouse. If a couple doesn't vow to be faithful for the rest of their lives or to be open to children, they cannot live out the full meaning of marriage.

When a husband and wife enter marriage, their home becomes like a little Church. Because their vocation is holy, the everyday tasks of marriage and family—like doing laundry, mowing the lawn, and even changing diapers—become holy, too. Husbands and wives can work together on becoming great saints by living out their vocation with self-giving love.

IF YOU ASK ME ...

- *The longest I have heard of a couple being married is _____ years.*

- *A couple who is a good example of married life is _____ and _____.*

Called to consecrated life

Another vocation is **consecrated life** as a religious sister, a nun, a religious brother, or a consecrated single person. Consecrated people also make vows, but their vows are to God, not a spouse. Those in consecrated life vow not to get married or own many possessions. This helps their hearts stay focused on loving God. It also gives them more time and energy for prayer and special work for God, such as serving the poor, running hospitals, traveling as missionaries, or living a life dedicated to prayer. They are like spiritual superheroes for the Church, offering hidden strength to the whole body of Christ through their faithful simplicity and prayer on our behalf.

People in consecrated life usually live in a community with others. There are hundreds of different communities with distinct ways of life, called **orders**, that fulfill different needs in the Church.

Like marriage, consecrated vocations require an unselfish self-gift to others and a lifelong commitment. This is one reason why a nun wears a veil: to symbolize that she is the "bride" of Christ, not of an earthly husband. This especially close union with Jesus is like a sneak preview of heaven, where every person will be united intimately with God.

There are many forms of consecrated life. If you feel interested in consecrated life, talk to someone who is living out that vocation. Here is a brief overview:

- Sisters, nuns, monks, brothers, and religious-order priests are part of *religious life*. In religious life, a community of brothers or sisters lives, works, prays, and has fun together.

- Other consecrated vocations are *consecrated virgins*, members of *secular institutes*, or other forms. In these vocations, men and women commit themselves to their local bishop and serve the Church as consecrated single people in the world. They may or may not live in community with others.

- Like all vocations, the call to consecrated life is a call to love. Consecrated people aren't people who couldn't find a spouse. Instead, they choose to love and serve God with an undivided heart and live entirely dedicated to Christ and the Church. They remind us all that we are destined for heaven.

IF YOU ASK ME ...

- *One valuable thing that consecrated people have more time for is*

  _____.

- *I think the best thing about religious life would be*

  _____.

Called to ordained life

Catholic priests and permanent deacons are ordained into a vocation called **Holy Orders.** Priests act *in persona Christi*, "in the person of Christ." This means the Holy Spirit works through them to continue Jesus' ministry through the Church today—preaching, teaching, serving, and healing. Like Jesus, Catholic priests commit their lives to the Church as their family. This is why priests are called "Father": they serve their family,

the Church, in the truly meaningful times of life. They celebrate weddings and baptize people. They give spiritual direction and help people through illness, divorce, trauma, addiction, job loss, and death.

Through the power of the Holy Spirit, priests bring the sacraments to us. At Mass, priests consecrate bread and wine into the Body and Blood of Christ so we can be close to Jesus. In Confession, priests absolve our sins so our souls can be healed. In the Anointing of the Sick, priests administer grace to help us endure suffering and receive God's healing grace.

IF YOU ASK ME ...

- *A priest who is a good example of the priesthood is*

  _____.

- *Something I am really thankful that priests do is*

  _____.

Discernment

Is God calling you? The answer is yes! But where?

First, do not be afraid! God's dream for your life will bring you more joy, peace, and satisfaction than any plan you could dream up yourself. Does that mean your vocation will always be easy, comfortable, and without suffering? No, because our earthly lives are a pilgrimage through an imperfect world to our true home in heaven. But God will not call you to a vocation that makes you miserable! Your true vocation will empower you to find blessing in life's highs and lows, its successes and failures, its triumphs and disappointments.

Second, don't stress about the details right now. God usually calls us to a particular vocation gradually. You don't have to know everything today, or even by high school or college. There's no deadline for God's dream. Your job is simple. Focus on learning to trust and listen to God.

Discernment is the process of discovering your vocation. The most important parts of discernment are asking God what he wants and listening to his response. To do this, you will need time for regular prayer, especially silent prayer. As you grow in discernment, strive every day to grow in virtue and love unselfishly.

> *Your true vocation will empower you to find blessing in life's highs and lows, its successes and failures, its triumphs and disappointments.*

The five Ls

Discernment also has a practical side. The five Ls—look, listen, learn, live, and love—are practical steps to help you discern:

- **LOOK** for Jesus in your ordinary life. Maybe you will see Jesus in someone who needs your help. Maybe you will see Jesus in volunteer work. When you are discerning your vocation, remember: the places where you find Jesus are the places you are called to be. Look for Jesus in your daily life and—when you see him—follow!

- **LISTEN** to God's voice. Life is filled with distractions and noise. We can't listen to God if we can't hear him. This means we have to listen on purpose. It means taking time for silence and prayer. How do you pray and listen? Here are three important ways:

  » *Read the Bible.* If we don't know God's Word, how can we know what he is saying to us?

  » *Go to Eucharistic Adoration.* Spend time with Jesus in the Eucharist, either near a tabernacle inside church or in an

Adoration chapel. Instead of talking or thinking, just listen quietly. What ideas, feelings, needs, and desires come up? Even just a few minutes of Adoration can be powerful.

> » *Listen for Jesus speaking through others.* Jesus often speaks to us through others, especially those who know us and love us, and even more through those people who are striving to be faithful Christians.

- **LEARN** your purpose. You can discover it by exploring your gifts and desires. To get a feel for how you would fit into different vocations, spend time exploring each one. Pay attention to married couples and parents. Visit a convent, monastery, or seminary. Talk to someone in consecrated single life.

- **LIVE** to the maximum, not the minimum, and you will find freedom and joy. Do volunteer work. Get more involved at your church. Join a youth group. Go on a retreat. Take a chance and try different things. Be virtuous, different, and bold. True Christian life is not boring, but an adventure. While the culture often promotes a life of pleasure and distraction, Jesus offers us a life of confidence and action. Living to the maximum will prepare you for the next step of the adventure.

- **LOVE** like God. This one is the most important. If you want to know your vocation,

> "Ignorance of the Scriptures is ignorance of Christ."
> —St. Jerome

you need to practice loving like God loves. That means loving with your whole heart, selflessly. The more we love others, the more we become our true selves. When we focus on others before ourselves and live for God by loving like he loves, we finally fulfill who he made us to be. If you learn to love like God in your daily life, then discerning your vocation will become an exciting adventure, not a stressful unknown.

As you discern, God will share with you what you need to know, when you need to know it. At the right time, God will make the next step clear and will give you the peace and courage to take that step. You will gradually see more and more, whether you are called to marriage, consecrated life, or the priesthood. You will understand more and more how to use your talents to serve God for as long as God calls you to be single.

Remember, you are unique and unrepeatable. God knows you and loves you even better than you know and love yourself. You can trust the One who loves you most.

IF YOU ASK ME ...

- *One place I find Jesus in my life is* _____.

- *Someone who lives to the maximum is* _____.

What about now?

How can you fit the five Ls into your everyday life?

- Start by committing to five minutes of prayer each morning. Identify a time when you can pray. Is it when you first open your eyes and look at a crucifix or religious artwork in your room? Is it in silence as you get ready for the day?
  - » A specific time every morning I can pray is _____.

- Spend quality time with your friends and family instead of isolating yourself on devices and screens. Play a board or card game, create something crafty, cook a new recipe, play sports, dance, play or listen to music, exercise, go for a walk, or just sit outside and talk. This can be an opportunity to look for Jesus and hear his voice.
  - » A specific activity I can do with my family or friends is _____.

- Each evening, review how well you lived out the five Ls. This takes only a few minutes and can be a prayerful way to fall asleep. Celebrate with Jesus whatever you did faithfully. Ask him to help you to do better tomorrow in areas where you fell short.
  - » A specific time every evening I can review my day is _____.

- Clear the noise. If we live with constant distractions, it is much harder to recognize and follow God's voice. For example, there's nothing wrong with watching uplifting shows, but watching them constantly is a problem. Any constant distraction sidetracks us from our real purpose.
  - » A specific way I can clear some noise from my life is _____.

- Practice being kind, considerate, attentive, forgiving, and helpful. Avoid negative humor or sarcastic insults that tear people down.

- Don't rush into dating. The purpose of dating is to find a spouse and discern the vocation of marriage. Are you ready to discern marriage? Instead of dealing with the pressure of serious dating, find peace and fun by spending time with friends.

- Choose chastity internally and externally. Sexual sins will add anxiety, pain, and obstacles to hearing God's voice. Chastity will empower you to focus on the right things and become who God knows you can be.

- Stay focused on virtue in all your relationships. The reward will be a much clearer and more hopeful vision of God's plan for you.

IF YOU ASK ME ...

- *I think the L I need to work on the most is _____.*

Quick Quiz

1. Holiness is for _____ everywhere, at every age.

2. Holy means _____ or _____.

3. A _____ is a path in life that will best fulfill your strengths, heal your weaknesses, and help you become a saint.

4. Three vocations in the Church are _____, _____, and _____.

5. True or False? There are many paths to holiness.

6. _____ is the process of discovering your vocation by asking God what he wants and listening to his response.

7. The five Ls are _____, _____, _____, _____, and _____.

 Video 3: Witness and Wrap-Up

Talents, Desires, and Discernment

Author and theologian Frederick Buechner was speaking of vocation when he said, "The place God calls you to is the place where your deep gladness and the world's deep hunger meet." One key to discernment is identifying the personal gifts God has given you. These may include abilities (like being a great writer or athlete) and strengths (like being a good listener or seeing the good in others). Talents are often connected to our desires, interests, and things that bring us joy.

Journal with the following reflection questions to help you identify your gifts:

- What are the things that other people come to you for (for example, help with homework, advice, amazing baked goods)?

- What do you love doing so much that you could do it for hours?

- What are some meaningful compliments that you have received over the years?

- What subjects do you love talking about?

- What brings you the greatest joy?

Got It?

- *LOOK for Jesus.*
- *LISTEN to God's voice.*
- *LEARN your purpose.*
- *LIVE to the maximum.*
- *LOVE like God.*

CLOSING PRAYER

+ In the name of the Father, and of the Son, and of the Holy Spirit. Amen.

In the divine image, Lord, you created him; male and female you created them. God our Father, you call each of us by name to be close to you and to be fully alive. Thank you for the people in our lives who teach us to faithfully follow your call. Help us eagerly listen and respond to your call, trusting that your plans are always best for us.

Jesus, your Mother Mary followed God's will in all things, so we turn to her now as we pray, *Hail Mary* ... Amen.

VOCABULARY

vocation: A calling from God to a particular path in life that will best fulfill your strengths, heal your weaknesses, and help you become a saint. Each person has a universal call to holiness that is received at Baptism. Vocations within the Church may include marriage, consecrated life, or Holy Orders.

marriage: A sacramental, holy bond, binding until death, between a baptized man and woman and God. Marriage calls for a free, total, faithful, and fruitful relationship that is open to bringing new life into the world. Marriage is a sign of Christ and the Church. A husband and wife are called to be a visible reminder of the love that Jesus has for his Bride, the Church, which is especially revealed in his Passion and Resurrection.

consecrated life: A vocation in which a man or a woman makes vows to God instead of to a spouse. Consecrated people do not marry or own many possessions so that they will have more time, energy, and focus to do special work for God. They often live in a community of others with the same call. Consecrated religious men are called "brothers" or "monks" while consecrated religious women are called "nuns" or "sisters."

religious orders: In consecrated life, orders are different religious communities with distinct ways of life that fulfill different needs in the Church.

Holy Orders: The sacrament received when a man is ordained as a priest, deacon, or bishop. Men who receive Holy Orders in the Roman Catholic Church have a special responsibility to be God's instruments by celebrating the sacraments and serving the people of God.

discernment: The process of discovering your vocation by asking God what he wants, listening to his response, and following him one step at a time.

Lesson Eight: The Adventure of "Yes"
LIVING OUT THE LANGUAGE OF THE BODY EVERY DAY

OPENING PRAYER

+ In the name of the Father, and of the Son, and of the Holy Spirit. Amen.

In the divine image, Lord, you created him; male and female you created them. Jesus, you make all things new. You call us to cooperate with your grace so you can set us free. Give us strength to make the life changes we need to make to be your true disciples.

Jesus, your Father gives us strength to change, even when it calls for new directions and new relationships, and so, in the Holy Spirit, we pray, *Our Father* ... Amen.

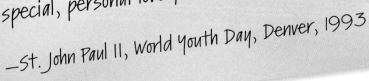

"I ask you to have the courage to commit yourselves to the truth. **Have the courage to believe the Good News about Life which Jesus teaches in the Gospel.** Open your minds and hearts to the beauty of all that God has made and to his special, personal love for each one of you."

—St. John Paul II, World Youth Day, Denver, 1993

THE BIG PICTURE

You've asked the big questions about who you are, where you're heading, and how you are going to get there. Now it's time to live out what you have discovered.

You know that life is so much more than checking off to-do lists while you wait for weekend fun. The real adventure is found in saying yes to God every day. God is calling you to trust him deeply. He is asking you to open your heart and mind to his vision and dream for your life. As each day begins, he invites you to live out that vision. How?

Make a commitment. Have a plan. Most importantly, be open to the grace and love that God wants to give you.

Yet again, I stood in line to confess the same sin. Leading up to Confession, I had fought a familiar battle in my mind. An inner voice repeated, *"If you were really sorry ... if you really wanted to do better ... you wouldn't have done it again. Why even bother now?"* It was a cold, harsh, bitter voice. But a second voice—clear, confident, and warm—said, *"Repent, strive, come back to me."*

So, once again, I chose to follow the second voice into the Confession line. I prayed and searched my heart. I reviewed the choices that had led me back into the familiar sin. As I reflected, I felt ashamed, discouraged, and sad. Why did I keep doing this? Sin was making me miserable, and I knew it. Why did I keep lying to myself in the moment that it was okay this time? As I moved forward in line, the knot in my stomach got tighter. I dreaded the moment I'd have to say my sin out loud, but I stayed in line. Eventually it was my turn.

"Bless me, Father, for I have sinned ..."

I confessed. I said what I had done out loud, admitting to the priest that I had confessed it many times before. Hot tears rolled down my cheeks. The priest was kind and strong. He challenged me, but in a way that made me feel stronger and braver. He gave me a penance and spoke the powerful words of absolution: "I absolve you of your sins in the name of the Father, and of the Son, and of the Holy Spirit." I received it, thanked him, let out a deep breath, and walked out. After I finished my penance, I just sat in church for a while.

That day was the last time I ever had to confess that particular sin. I can't explain exactly how, but something changed that day. At each of the dozens of confessions before that one, I had been truly sorry. I had been serious about avoiding sin, and then failed again anyway. But that day, my commitment and striving met with the mysterious timing of God's gift of grace. I was finally free.

Imagine if I had given up just before that confession. Imagine if I had listened to the cold, harsh voice telling me it was pointless. How deeply would I have become enslaved to my sin? Striving and repenting, again and again if necessary, opens us up more and more to receiving God's grace. Grace restores us and, in God's timing, sets us free.

At World Youth Day 2000 in Italy, St. John Paul II reminded us never to give up, because God is with us: "Dear young people, in these noble undertakings you are not alone. ... In the struggle against sin you are not alone: so many like you are struggling and through the Lord's grace are winning!"

Knowing who we are, where we're headed, and how we get there doesn't mean that we instantly become perfect. But the clear, confident, warm voice of God calls us to commitment and recommitment, again and again, as many times as necessary. God's grace changes everything.—*Colin MacIver*

IF YOU ASK ME ...

- *Three things that I am committed to are:*

  _____

  _____

  _____

- *Something I want to get better at is* _____.

- *Someone who is a model of striving and commitment is* _____.

Video 1: Introduction

IF YOU ASK ME ...

- *To me, true happiness is* _____.

Video 2: To the Core

VIDEO QUESTIONS

1. **True or False:** Charles Blondin's manager decided not to go across the tightrope.

2. **True or False:** Telling the truth will bring you freedom.

3. **True or False:** The person who stays with the crowd is the one with the best story.

Committing to live God's way is a big step, but nothing makes more sense. God has given his own Son to save us. He is already totally committed to us, even before we respond to him. He is waiting at the door of our hearts, ready to give us the best. But the door to our hearts can be opened only from the inside. Saying yes to God opens the door to the blessings he wants to give us.

Living God's way is a lifetime goal that we grow in every day. Think about any long-term dream you have. No dream becomes reality by staying exactly where you are now. No dream becomes reality all at once, either. If you want to go somewhere on vacation, you won't get there by sitting in the parked car in the driveway. And you can't just teleport there in an instant. You have to start moving and keep moving toward your destination. The destination unfolds step by step, mile by mile.

It's the same in our relationships, love, and vocation. We follow God by taking action and saying yes to specific choices, one moment at a time. The

Theology of the Body helps us learn how to say yes. It helps us be faithful with the language of our bodies—faithful to the great adventure of love and holiness. We become more fluent in this language of the body as we grow in virtue and receive grace through the sacraments. Saying yes to the love of God and others is the only path to lasting joy.

IF YOU ASK ME ...

- *Who are three people or activities you have made a commitment to?*

- *I'm glad I made a commitment to _____ because _____.*

An embodied faith

Have you ever noticed how your faith is connected to your body? Because the spiritual world is invisible, sometimes we think of our faith as something mental, not physical. Yet our Catholic Faith connects to both the body and the body's language. The Eucharist is not bread but the *Body* of Christ. The Church is not a building with a steeple and pews but the *Body* of Christ. Jesus "spoke" his love for us through the language of his body on the Cross. He continues to speak his love for us through the language of his Body in the Church, especially through the sacraments.

The sacraments flow from Christ through the Church, expressing God's invisible love through words and signs that we experience. The sacraments show the connection between faith and the body. When you receive a sacrament, what you experience in your body reveals what God is doing in your soul.

At Baptism, for example, the water poured over your head is a visible sign of the grace cleansing your soul and making you a child of God. When you participate in Mass, your body speaks worship of God: genuflecting, making the Sign of the Cross, standing for the Gospel, and kneeling during the Consecration. When you receive Communion, your body—and therefore your soul—is united with Jesus in the Eucharist. When the bishop traces blessed oil onto your forehead at Confirmation, your soul is sealed with the power to live and share your faith. The sacraments continue to reveal your relationship with God through the language of the body.

Through the Church and the sacraments, God says that he loves us, is committed to us, and wants what is best for us. He invites us to return that love and commitment through the language of our bodies.

So how do we live out the Theology of the Body in everyday life?

True friendship speaks through the language of your body. True friends are like teammates on a gold-medal team. True friends help each other become the best people they can be, even when it's tough. They challenge and support each other toward the goal of practicing virtue. They encourage each other in weak moments. They applaud each other's achievements, support each other when things go wrong, and eventually win … *together*.

This is so much better than the back-stabbing and drama that sometimes happen at school and in sports. We have all seen "friendships" that are nothing more than participating together in destructive, negative actions like bullying, gossiping, name-calling, drinking, disobeying, or partying. These "friendships" tear people down instead of building them up.

Bad peer pressure makes it hard to break free from destructive, false "friendships." When someone brags about doing something wrong, you might not say anything because you're afraid of being labeled. Sometimes bad peer pressure is less of a spoken thing and more of a feeling. Maybe you join in doing something destructive just because it seems like everyone around you is doing it, too.

Is that what you really want in your friendships: pressure, bullying, and the anxiety of being labeled? Are you just looking for company in your bad habits, or do you want friends who help you and one another become better?

Speak the truth with the language of your body in friendship. Be a true friend. Instead of dragging others down into bad habits, treat them with respect. Instead of insulting or making fun of them, honor people who don't give in to bad peer pressure. Choose friends not for how popular they are but for how much they treat others with the dignity of being made in God's own image and likeness.

IF YOU ASK ME …

- *Someone who is a true friend is* _____.

- *Someone I would like to be better friends with is* _____.

Family love speaks the truth

Our families are important—so important that they even have their own commandment: "Honor your mother and your father." The family is sometimes called "the domestic church." This means that in this little church, families are called to be visible signs of God's unconditional love. By remaining committed to each other through good times and bad, family members reflect God's eternal commitment. By loving and sacrificing for each other, family members reflect God's unconditional love.

What does this look like for you? How do you express God's love in the language of your body? Maybe it's listening to your sister after she's had a hard day. Maybe it's playing with your brother instead of staying in your room. Maybe it's helping your parents make dinner or asking them about work. All these things reflect God's concern for every aspect of our lives.

At the same time, you know all too well that your parents and siblings aren't perfect. Have you ever noticed that sometimes family members treat each other worse than they treat total strangers? And our families are usually those we love most! Why do you think this happens?

Many families experience struggles. Many families go through tough times. Many families argue or sometimes say hurtful things. Because you're so aware of your family's flaws, it can be easy to lose your patience or get annoyed with them. Sometimes it takes even more effort to love your family than it does to love anyone else! Even St. Teresa of Calcutta said, "Sometimes it is harder for us to smile at those who live with us, the immediate members of our family, than it is to smile at those who are not so close to us."

Some families deal with painful issues like job loss, serious illness, trauma, divorce, abuse, addiction, and death. But no matter what pain a family may experience, God loves each family member and wants to heal every wound. Even if your family has disappointed you or hurt you, the Father's love for you will never change. As God's son or daughter, you are part of a safe, stable, eternal family that nothing can break.

You "speak" love for your family through the language of your body. Whenever you help your parents around the house, speak kindly to your siblings, apologize for your mistakes, and forgive the mistakes of others, your actions speak love

"Sometimes it is harder for us to smile at those who live with us, the immediate members of our family, than it is to smile at those who are not so close to us."

and commitment. You have real power—the power to help your family understand and experience the even greater love and commitment of God. Being a visible sign of God's love in the family may begin with you.

IF YOU ASK ME ...

- *One "high" of my family is* _____.

- *One "low" of my family is* _____.

- *Something about my family that I am grateful for is* _____.

Chastity speaks the truth

The virtue of chastity empowers our bodies to speak love and commitment in the way that matches the truth of our relationships. Remember that chastity is not just saying no to sex (abstinence). Chastity is saying yes to choices that reflect unselfish love. These include speaking respectfully, dressing and behaving modestly, and treating others the way you want your future spouse to be treated. Chastity also means that we watch, listen to, post, and share things that build others up, and we never treat them like objects.

You can also practice chastity by praying for your future vocation. Yes, that means now! Whether God calls you to marriage, ordained life, or consecrated life, you can pray now for those you will be called to love and serve. The people connected to your future vocation will be affected by your choices today. Start loving them now with your choices and prayers.

Helping others speaks the truth

Speaking truth with the language of your body goes beyond your family, friends, and future. How did Jesus spend most of his time? His earthly ministry focused on people who had serious needs. He healed people who were disabled and sick. He accepted people who were rejected, mistreated, and cast out. He listened to people who felt alone and hopeless.

We should imitate Jesus. Maybe you can't heal someone's illness, but you can invite someone lonely to sit with you at lunch. You can volunteer at a food bank, visit a nursing home, or participate in activities at your parish. The Church outlines for us fourteen corporal (bodily) and spiritual works of mercy (see sidebar). The corporal acts in particular show the love of Christ to others through the language of the body.

When you help and serve others, you grow too. Your relationship with Jesus deepens. Through the language of your body, you allow God to speak to others. If you are open, who knows what wonderful things God can do and say through you?

Corporal Works of Mercy
Feed the hungry
Give drink to the thirsty
Clothe the naked
Shelter the homeless
Visit the sick
Visit prisoners
Bury the dead

Spiritual Works of Mercy
Instruct the ignorant
Counsel the doubtful
Admonish sinners
Bear wrongs patiently
Forgive offenses willingly
Comfort the afflicted
Pray for the living and the dead

IF YOU ASK ME ...

- *One work of mercy that I can do this week is* _____.

- *I can do this work of mercy by* _____.

"Be not afraid"

The most repeated message in the whole Bible—the Old Testament and the New Testament together—is "Fear not" and "Be not afraid." In fact, this message is repeated even more than the message to *love*.

Why? Think about all the ways fear prevents us from doing things God's way—the best way. We are afraid that we will fail a test, so we are tempted to cheat. Not God's way. We are afraid that people will make fun of us, so we are tempted to participate in gossip. Not God's way. We are afraid that nobody likes us, so we are tempted to use our bodies to attract attention. Not God's way.

Sometimes we are afraid of committing our lives to God. What will happen? Will we lose something? What will God ask us to do? What will we have to surrender to him? If following God means sacrificing and putting others first, what will we have to give up? Sometimes we might fear that if we follow God's way, we will miss out on all the fun.

But being afraid of God doesn't add up. God wants to give you only good things. He's your biggest fan. God's greatest desire is for you to experience true happiness and love through a relationship with him. Only God can empower you to love yourself and others with real love. This is the only path to real fulfillment in your life—and, eventually, forever in heaven. Jesus does not want fear to rule our lives, but love! The good news is that "there is no fear in love, but perfect love casts out fear" (1 John 4:18). Overcoming fear is an important step to real, self-giving love.

In his first days as pope, St. John Paul II told the Church, "Be not afraid!" He knew that fear is just a waste of time and energy, so he rejected fear and turned to God's love. He continued this message throughout his papacy, especially to encourage young people: "My dear young people, only Jesus knows what is in your hearts and your deepest desires. Only He, who has loved you to the end (cf. Jn 13:1), can fulfill your aspirations. His are words of eternal life, words that give meaning to life. No one apart from Christ can give you true happiness."

We should not be afraid, because Jesus came to save us. Jesus said, "I came that they may have life, and have it abundantly" (John 10:10). *Abundant* means far beyond the minimum. When you have something abundantly, you have way more than enough.

Jesus is all about abundance. When he multiplied the fishes and loaves for a hungry crowd, the people received way more than they needed.

Several thousand people ate until they were full, and the leftovers still filled twelve baskets (John 6:11–13). Jesus provided abundantly for their needs—way more than anyone could ever expect.

No matter who has disappointed you in your life, Jesus will always keep his promises and exceed your hopes and dreams. You can trust the one who knows you best. You can trust the one who loves you most. You can trust the one who died to give you life.

Are you ready for the adventure of following him?

IF YOU ASK ME ...

- *I used to be afraid of _____ but now I'm not.*

- *I want to conquer my fear of _____.*

Quick Quiz

1. Our Catholic Faith connects to our _____ and the _____ of the body.

2. When you receive a _____, what you experience in your body reveals what God is doing in your soul.

3. The family is so important to our spiritual growth that it even has its own commandment: "Honor your _____ and _____."

4. You have the power to help your family experience _____.

5. You can practice chastity by _____ for your future vocation.

6. We should imitate Jesus by doing the corporal works of _____.

7. The most repeated idea in the New Testament is "_____."

 Video 3: Witness and Wrap-Up

Commitment

Join your Theology of the Body leader and group in praying and making the following commitment together.

+ In the name of the Father, and of the Son, and of the Holy Spirit. Amen.

Invite a volunteer to read Romans 12:1–2:

"I urge you therefore, brothers, by the mercies of God, to offer your bodies as a living sacrifice, holy and pleasing to God, your spiritual worship. Do not conform yourselves to this age but be transformed by the renewal of your mind, that you may discern what is the will of God, what is good and pleasing and perfect" (NAB).

Read the pledge together:

- I promise, with the help of God's grace, to live my baptismal call through a commitment to chastity.
- I promise, with the help of God's grace, to learn to speak the truth through the language of my body.
- I reject the false promises of the world, and I trust in God's plan for me and my future.
- I pledge to strive for purity in the way that I live.
- I pledge to be a faithful friend, following Christ and supporting others through generosity and sacrifice.
- I pledge to seek forgiveness, strength, and healing in the sacraments.
- I want to receive all that God has in store for me.

Pray together:

Glory Be ... Amen.

Got It?

Commit to the truth.

Rely on God's grace.

Obey God's law.

Strive and sacrifice for love.

Step out in faith.

CLOSING PRAYER

+ In the name of the Father, and of the Son, and of the Holy Spirit. Amen.

In the divine image, Lord, you created him; male and female you created them. God, you are so faithful. Like a Good Shepherd you will give us courage, care for us, and protect us until we are with you forever. Help us to trust that your goodness and kindness will lead us *and* follow us all the days of our lives.

Jesus, your mother always trusted your goodness, so we turn to her now as we pray, *Hail Mary* ... Amen.

FINISH STRONG

Our restless hearts seek beyond our limits, challenging our capacity to think and love: to think and love the immeasurable, the infinite, the absolute and supreme form of Being. Our inner eye looks upon the unlimited horizons of our hopes and aspirations. And in the midst of all life's contradictions, we seek the true meaning of life. We wonder, and we ask ourselves:

Who am I? Where am I going? How do I get there?

We all ask ourselves these questions. Humanity in its entirety feels the pressing need to give meaning and purpose to a world in which being happy is increasingly difficult and complex. The bishops of the whole world who gathered at the Second Vatican Council expressed it as follows:

"In the face of modern developments there is a growing body of people who are asking the most fundamental of all questions or are glimpsing them with a keener insight: What is humanity? What is the meaning of suffering, evil, death, which have not been eliminated by all this progress? ... What can people contribute to society? What can they expect from it? What happens after this earthly life is ended?" —*Gaudium et Spes* 10

St. John Paul II put it like this:

"Failure to ask these basic questions means renouncing the great adventure of seeking the truth about life."—*St. John Paul II, World Youth Day, Denver, 1993*

Further Resources

Catholic Prayers

You may already know some of these prayers. Practice one or two every day. When you've memorized them, you'll be able to pray them anytime—at Mass, when you say the Rosary, when you or a friend needs help, and whenever you want to say thank you to God.

Our Father

Our Father, who art in heaven, hallowed be thy name.
Thy kingdom come. Thy will be done, on earth as it is in heaven.
Give us this day our daily bread, and forgive us our trespasses,
as we forgive those who trespass against us.
And lead us not into temptation, but deliver us from evil. Amen.

Hail Mary

Hail Mary, full of grace, the Lord is with thee.
Blessed art thou among women, and blessed is the fruit of thy womb, Jesus.
Holy Mary, Mother of God, pray for us sinners,
now and at the hour of our death. Amen.

Glory Be

Glory be to the Father, and to the Son, and to the Holy Spirit, as it was in the beginning, is now, and ever shall be, world without end. Amen.

Apostles' Creed

I believe in God, the Father almighty, Creator of heaven and earth, and in Jesus Christ, his only Son, our Lord, who was conceived by the Holy Spirit, born of the Virgin Mary, suffered under Pontius Pilate, was crucified, died and was buried; he descended into hell; on the third day he rose again from the dead; he ascended into heaven, and is seated at the right hand of God the Father almighty; from there he will come to judge the living and the dead. I believe in the Holy Spirit, the holy catholic Church, the communion of saints, the forgiveness of sins, the resurrection of the body, and life everlasting. Amen.

Fatima Prayer

O my Jesus, forgive us our sins, save us from the fires of hell, and lead all souls to heaven, especially those in most need of your mercy.

Hail, Holy Queen

Hail, Holy Queen, Mother of Mercy, our life, our sweetness, and our hope. To thee do we cry, poor banished children of Eve. To thee do we send up our sighs, mourning and weeping in this valley of tears. Turn, then, most gracious advocate, thine eyes of mercy toward us, and after this our exile, show unto us the blessed fruit of thy womb, Jesus. O clement, O loving, O sweet Virgin Mary.

V. Pray for us, O Holy Mother of God.

R. That we may be made worthy of the promises of Christ. Amen.

Rosary Prayer

O God, whose only begotten Son, by his life, death, and Resurrection, has purchased for us the rewards of eternal life, grant, we beseech thee, that while meditating on these mysteries of the Most Holy Rosary of the Blessed Virgin Mary, we may imitate what they contain and obtain what they promise, through the same Christ our Lord. Amen.

Prayer to St. Michael

St. Michael the Archangel, defend us in battle;
be our protection against the wickedness and snares of the devil.
May God rebuke him, we humbly pray.
And do thou, O Prince of the heavenly host, by the power of God,
cast into hell Satan and all the evil spirits
who prowl through the world seeking the ruin of souls. Amen.

Act of Contrition

O my God,
I am heartily sorry for having offended you,
and I detest all my sins, because of your just punishments
but most of all because they offend you, my God,
who are all good and deserving of all my love.
I firmly resolve, with the help of your grace,
to sin no more
and to avoid the near occasions of sin. Amen.

Grace Before Meals

Bless us, O Lord, and these thy gifts
which we are about to receive from thy bounty
through Christ our Lord. Amen.

The Rosary

The Rosary gives us a chance to spend time with Our Lady and think about the events of Jesus' life, death, and Resurrection. For each mystery, imagine yourself in the scene, and ask Mary to help you see Jesus with her eyes. The Rosary is a beautiful way to pray with Mary on your own, with your family, and with friends.

Rosary beads are special. They may look like a necklace, but we don't wear them. We hold them in our hands and keep count of the prayers with our fingers, always treating the beads with respect and affection.

THE MYSTERIES OF THE ROSARY

The Joyful Mysteries
1. The Annunciation
2. The Visitation
3. The Nativity
4. The Presentation
5. The Finding of Jesus in the Temple

The Luminous Mysteries
1. The Baptism of Christ in the Jordan
2. The Manifestation of Christ at the Wedding of Cana
3. The Proclamation of the Kingdom of God
4. The Transfiguration
5. The Institution of the Eucharist

The Sorrowful Mysteries
1. The Agony in the Garden
2. The Scourging at the Pillar
3. The Crowning with Thorns
4. The Carrying of the Cross
5. The Crucifixion

The Glorious Mysteries
1. The Resurrection
2. The Ascension
3. The Descent of the Holy Spirit
4. The Assumption
5. The Coronation of the Blessed Virgin Mary

HOW TO PRAY THE ROSARY

For the text of the individual prayers listed here, see "Catholic Prayers" above.

1. Holding the rosary beads, make the Sign of the Cross.

2. Pray the Apostles' Creed (on the crucifix).

3. Pray an Our Father (first bead).

4. Pray three Hail Marys (second through fourth beads).

5. Pray the Glory Be and the (optional) Fatima Prayer (fifth bead).

6. Announce the first mystery, and then pray the Our Father.

7. Pray ten Hail Marys on the next decade (ten beads), meditating on the mystery.

8. On the next single bead, pray the Glory Be and the (optional) Fatima Prayer.

9. On the same bead, announce the next mystery and pray the Our Father.

10. Repeat steps 7 to 9 for each of the four remaining mysteries.

11. After the fifth mystery, pray the Hail, Holy Queen (on the rosary centerpiece).

12. Conclude with the Rosary Prayer, and make the Sign of the Cross.

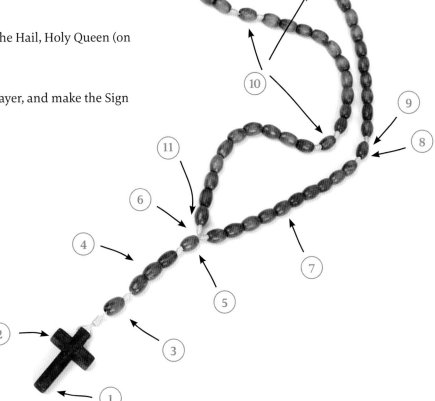

Additional Lesson Activities

Lesson One

Unique and Unrepeatable Me

Create a collage or self-portrait of images that represent your uniqueness. Put the images together in a slide presentation, a collage, or some other artistic piece. Images may be hand-drawn or digital. Include one image that represents each of the following elements:

- A personality trait that makes people laugh
- A personality trait your friends value most about you
- A secret talent or weird ability
- Something good you have done for someone else
- A favorite "something" (be original—no people, songs, movies, foods, animals, or colors!)
- Three blessings God has given you
- Quotes from three different family members, friends, and teachers describing something they love, appreciate, or admire about you (don't quote the same person twice!)

Media Mash-Up

Create a playlist of five to ten songs or video clips that you believe capture the challenging process of growing up. Explain your choices in a brief paragraph or present your playlist to the group or class.

Lesson Two

Genesis Theater

Produce a skit that acts out the story of Genesis 3. Your leader or teacher will break you up into groups and give you a few props that you must use in your skit. You can reenact the biblical story or make up a modern-day version.

Presenting Genesis

Create an Adam-and-Eve video short, slide show, or comic strip illustrating the lie that Satan told Adam and Eve.

Genesis, Dr. Seuss Style

Create a children's story of Creation in a way that would make Dr. Seuss proud. Focus especially on the creation, temptation, and Fall of Adam and Eve. Express the truth of Genesis clearly while using your imagination and creativity to make it come alive in a new way.

Heaven Road Trip

Plan an imaginary road trip to our ultimate destiny of heaven. Create a slideshow or other presentation to share the following items:

- Who would you choose as a road trip buddy to help you get to heaven? Why?

- What three songs would you add to a playlist for this road trip to heaven? Why?

- What are three places you would stop along the way to help you prepare for heaven? Why?

Freedom Essay

Adam and Eve misused their freedom, but St. John Paul II stated, "Freedom exists for the sake of love." Write an essay exploring this question: *How would the world be different over the last hundred years if just five influential community, national, and world leaders used their freedom for the sake of love? Which male leaders come to mind? Which female leaders come to mind? Why?*

Lesson Three

Silent Skits

Perform a skit that tells the story of Jesus' life using a song melody and body language only—no words!

Comic Strip

Make a comic strip that tells a story without words, only pictures. Trade comics with a friend, but don't tell each other what your comics are about. Write what you think is happening in each other's comics, and then compare to see if the stories match what the comics' creator had in mind.

Human Person Campaign

Create a PSA (public service announcement) that teaches people the true value and meaning of the human body. You may choose to create a video, a series of social media posts, a set of posters, a short ad, etc.

"My Body Says" Essay

Answer and explain: What did God create our bodies to say? Why? Use at least one quote from the chapter to support your answer.

Language-of-the-Body Art

Create a symbolic artwork that represents the language of the body, then share with your group. You may create the artwork on your own or with a small group. Illustrate the following body parts. On each body part, show the answer to the associated question with pictures, words, shapes, colors, or symbols.

- *Hair:* What are three statements about love that you find meaningful (Scriptures, quotes, song lyrics, definitions, movie lines, notes from class, etc.)?
- *Eyes:* How should you look at another person?
- *Mouth:* What words should be spoken to show authentic love?
- *Ears:* What are the most important messages about love that the world needs to hear?
- *Arms:* What are some physical ways that love is expressed?
- *Hands:* What gifts can you personally offer to others?
- *Legs:* What characteristics do you want in friends who can walk through life with you?
- *Feet:* What is the foundation of real love?

Lesson Four

Growing in Virtue

Theological Virtues	Cardinal Virtues
faith	prudence
hope	justice
charity	fortitude
	temperance

In the box is a list of the theological and cardinal virtues. Write down one particular virtue that you would like to grow in. For the next five days, practice this virtue. Although it will definitely take more time to establish the virtue, five days is a good start! _____

Write the name of someone who can help you grow in your virtue. Once a day for the five project days, have your partner ask how your practice is going. _____

Write three specific things you can do every day to grow in your virtue. Choose specific actions like "Take out the trash without being asked," "Get up when my alarm rings so my parents don't have to yell," or "Instead of spending time on devices, spend time helping my family."

1. _____

2. _____

3. _____

Fill in the chart at the end of each day:

	DAY 1	DAY 2	DAY 3	DAY 4	DAY 5
Check in with partner					
Daily practice: describe what you did					
Successes					
Challenges					
Any thoughts or insights?					

On Day 5, answer the following questions, and discuss your experience with your TOB group.

1. If I were to describe how I was progressing in virtue, what would I say about myself?

2. From this experiment, what did I learn about myself?

3. In the future, what should I do to grow in my virtue?

4. How much did my partner help me?

5. What are my overall feelings about doing this experiment?

Making Virtue Practical

Review the descriptions of the four cardinal virtues below: prudence, justice, fortitude, and temperance. Pick two of the four that are difficult for you. Then write a few paragraphs about one or two people you know who live those virtues well and what you can learn from their example.

- **Prudence** is determining what is best in a particular situation and choosing to do what is best, even when it may be inconvenient.

- **Justice** is giving people what they deserve as human persons. It is *just* for us to worship and thank God, because he deserves worship and gratitude. It is *just* to give food to the poor, because as human persons the poor deserve what they need to survive.

- **Fortitude** is continuing toward the good even when we want to quit, like overcoming exhaustion to keep studying for your exams, or finishing yard work to help your family, even though it's blazing hot outside.

- **Temperance** is enjoying good things the right way, and not letting our desires control us. For example, chastity is a virtue related to temperance, because chastity helps us direct our sexuality toward love, not just pleasure.

Lesson Five

Growing Up

Who is an adult in your parish, school, or community who shows what it means to be a man or woman of God? Make a thank-you card or write an encouraging letter to this person for showing you what a disciple looks like.

Advice

Select a character from the fictional case study that your leader provides for you. Write a message giving the character advice about what to do in his or her situation. Include three things you learned from this chapter in your advice.

Love Story

Pick a movie that you think is a great example of a real love story, showing commitment and willingness to sacrifice. Write a paragraph explaining three ways you think this movie shows love.

People and Things

Create a slideshow, poster, collage, or some other visual that illustrates three ways our culture loves things and uses people (when it should be the other way around). Make sure illustrations are appropriate.

Love Playlist

Create a playlist of ten songs that capture what real love looks like and how it acts. Share your playlist and explain your choices. Highlight the lyrics that best represent or describe true love!

Works of Mercy

Authentic holiness means making a gift of ourselves in everyday circumstances to God and others. If we pay attention, we will find that our days are packed with opportunities. Review the fourteen works of mercy and choose three to do this week.

Remember, the works of mercy are not always literal. For example, "giving drink to the thirsty" may be getting a refill for a friend; "counseling the doubtful" may be really listening to someone in conversation; "admonishing sinners" may be reminding your friends not to use bad language or insulting jokes.

After your experience, answer these reflection questions:

- Which works of mercy did you fulfill or try to fulfill?
- How long did it take you to find opportunities for works of mercy?
- How did people respond to your works of mercy?
- How did you feel before, during and after fulfilling your works of mercy?

Future Discernment Letter

Answer the following questions in a letter to yourself. Ask someone reliable to keep your letter and then send it to you in one year. When you receive your letter one year from now, reflect on how well you have lived out your discernment goals.

- What kind of person do I want to be?

- What fears do I want to conquer?

- What are my dreams? List them for the different areas of your life:

   » Personal _____

   » Spiritual _____

   » Relationships _____

Lesson Eight

Saintly Adventure

Look through this list of saints. Select one (or select your patron saint or another saint whom you find interesting) and research his or her life. Create a slideshow that highlights three to five details about this saint that inspire you to live out your own call to holiness.

- St. Josephine Bakhita

- St. Kateri Tekakwitha

- St. Lorenzo Ruiz

- St. Gianna Beretta Molla

- Bl. Carlo Acutis

- Ven. Augustus Tolton

- St. Oscar Romero

- Bl. Pier Giorgio Frassati

- St. Maria Goretti

- St. Jacinta Marto

- St. Paul Miki

- Ven. Pierre Toussaint

- Bl. Miguel Pro

- St. Clare of Assisi

- St. Agnes

- St. Cecilia

- St. Zelie Martin

- St. Joseph

- Bl. Columba Kang Wan-suk

Time Capsule

Create a time capsule of inspiration from this program to encourage you in your commitment to living the Theology of the Body. Keep the time capsule in a safe place that you can access in the years to come. Include the following items in a large envelope or small container:

- A quote from this program that inspired you

- A Scripture passage that will help you remember God's plan for life and love

- An encouraging note or two from your Theology of the Body group members and leaders

- Anything else that inspires you: artwork, holy cards, religious medals, etc.

Top Five+Five List

Write a list of five things that you learned in this program that you really want to remember. Then, for each of your top five things, list one way that you can truly live it out.

Glossary

abstinence: Refraining from something, such as abstaining from meat on Fridays in Lent. In relationships, abstinence is refraining from intimate sexual activity outside of marriage. Abstinence is a necessary part of chastity for unmarried people, but abstinence by itself is not the same as chastity.

adultery: The sin of sexual activity between a married person and someone who is not his or her spouse.

agape: The form of love that genuinely wants what is good for the other and works to achieve it. *Agape* isn't focused on self and gives without expecting anything in return. *Agape* inspires us to make sacrifices for those we love.

Ascension: After the Resurrection, Jesus literally went up (ascended) body and soul to heaven. He is in heaven now in a constant offering of love. One day, he will return to earth again in glory to bring us to live with him forever.

body language: Gestures and expressions that communicate inner thoughts and feelings.

cardinal virtues: *Cardinal* means "hinge," so the cardinal virtues—prudence, justice, fortitude, and temperance—are like hinges that open the door to other natural virtues as well.

chastity: A virtue that empowers us to love ourselves and others rightly through the language of our bodies. Chastity means living our sexuality in the way that tells the truth about our identity, vocation, and relationships throughout our lives; it also means striving for purity of mind, heart, and body. Chastity is a virtue for everyone in all vocations.

complementarity: The unique, different characteristics of maleness and femaleness created by God as a gift to bring out the best in each other and call us to communion and self-gift.

concupiscence: After the loss of grace in Original Sin, we have a tendency toward sin and selfishness. This tendency is caused by our damaged desires, which are called concupiscence.

consecrated life: A vocation in which a man or a woman makes vows to God instead of to a spouse. Consecrated people do not marry or own many possessions so that they will have more time, energy, and focus to do special work for God. They often live in a community of others with the same call. Consecrated religious men are called "brothers" or "monks" while consecrated religious women are called "nuns" or "sisters."

discernment: The process of discovering your vocation by asking God what he wants, listening to his response, and following him one step at a time.

eros: The form of love that wants to be close to the person you love. *Eros* must always be balanced with *agape* to protect it from selfishness or possessiveness.

Eucharist: Also called Holy Communion, the Eucharist is the greatest sacrament because it is literally Jesus himself—Body and Blood, Soul and Divinity. When the priest prays the Consecration at Mass, the bread and wine look the same but they become Jesus himself.

fornication: The sin of sexual activity between people who are not married.

free will: God created us with the ability to choose so that we are able to love. This ability to choose is necessary because love must be freely chosen and given. God wanted us to love him and each other, so he gave us free will.

grace: God's free gift of divine life in us, which was won for us by Jesus and which we receive especially through the sacraments. Like spiritual electricity for our souls, grace empowers us to live out virtues, .

habit: An action repeated so often that it becomes a natural part of a person's character.

Holy Orders: The sacrament received when a man is ordained as a priest, deacon, or bishop. Men who receive Holy Orders in the Roman Catholic Church have a special responsibility to be God's instruments by celebrating the sacraments and serving the people of God.

human person: God created human persons in his image and likeness for our own sake—just so he could love us and we could return that love. Every human person is made unique and unrepeatable, male or female, with a body and soul.

in his image and likeness: Human persons are created to reflect the love of the Trinity. The Trinity is three Persons in one God—Father, Son, and Holy Spirit—who eternally give themselves to each other in love. We are meant to do the same so that when we are in loving relationships, we understand more about God.

in the beginning: In the Garden of Eden, God created the first human persons fully able to live his plan of happiness for them. The way God originally created Adam and Eve is the way human beings were designed to live.

Incarnation: The Incarnation refers to Jesus, who is fully God, becoming fully man. God the Son became man to reveal the truth of our humanity and save us from the destruction caused by sin.

language of the body: The major Theology of the Body teaching is that the human body makes visible what is invisible. The body speaks a language without words about our human nature, purpose, and destiny. Jesus shows us that the body reveals a call to total self-gift.

lust: A vice that sees people as objects to be used rather than persons to be loved. Lust distorts sex into an expression of selfishness instead of self-gift. Lust damages our understanding of our true identity.

"Male and female he created them": This phrase from Genesis 1 reveals that from the beginning, God designed sex to communicate the love between a husband and wife in the relationship of marriage.

marriage: A sacramental, holy bond, binding until death, between a baptized man and woman and God. Marriage calls for a free, total, faithful, and fruitful relationship that is open to bringing new life into the world. Marriage is a sign of Christ and the Church. A husband and wife are called to be a visible reminder of the love that Jesus has for his Bride, the Church, which is especially revealed in his Passion and Resurrection.

modesty: A virtue that empowers us to respect the dignity of our bodies and God's design for sexuality in how we dress, speak, and act. Modesty expresses the reality that our goodness and beauty don't come from getting attention with our appearance or outward behavior but from being loved by God and from being ourselves the way he made us to be.

Original Sin: Original Sin refers to Adam and Eve's sin and its damaging effect on all of humanity. God designed human nature with the grace of holiness and the ability to choose what is good. Original Sin is the loss of this grace. Original Sin damages our ability to know what is right, choose what is good, and love; it causes us to suffer and even die; and it makes us tend to commit sin, even when we try not to.

pornography: Anything that includes images, videos, or written material intended to arouse lust.

Reconciliation: Also called Confession, the Sacrament of Reconciliation allows us to repent for our sins and have our souls wiped clean. Jesus is the one who absolves our sins; priests are his instruments in Confession. When we confess our sins to a priest, it is like talking directly to Jesus himself.

religious orders: In consecrated life, orders are different religious communities with distinct ways of life that fulfill different needs in the Church.

Resurrection: After his death on the Cross, Jesus rose from the dead. His human body and soul were reunited. Jesus' Resurrection opened for us the possibility of resurrection, when our own bodies and souls will reunite after death.

sacrament: Sacraments are visible signs of invisible realities that bring grace to our souls. Sacraments are administered through the Church.

saint: A saint is someone who has lived a holy life, practiced virtue to a heroic degree, and chosen to love God above all things. Saints come from every place, ethnicity, circumstance, and background. Saints may be priests or nuns, married, single, or even children. The Catholic Church canonizes (gives the title "Saint" to) these holy people to offer us examples of how we, too, should live. We are all called to live holy lives.

Satan: Satan was an angel who rejected God's will. He became the enemy of love and tempted Adam and Eve to sin. He is called "the father of lies" because he tempts us to sin with false promises of happiness.

sex: Sex is first about our identity as male or female created in God's image and likeness. Sex also refers to acts of physical intimacy between a husband and wife, especially intercourse. Sex expresses spouses' invisible gift of self and union with each other through the visible gift and union of their bodies. As marriage is a free, total, faithful, and fruitful union, sex is a free, total, faithful bodily union that has the potential fruitfulness of new life.

shame: The experience of Adam and Eve after the Fall, and all of us since then, fearing others as a threat to our dignity. At the same time, shame reminds us to recognize and protect our value.

sin: Sin is the choice not to follow God's laws. When we sin, we do something God says we should not do or we fail to do something God says we should do. Sin is a failure to love God and others.

spousal: Relating to or shared between a husband and a wife.

theological virtues: The theological virtues are faith, hope, and love. "Theological" means these virtues are given to us by God and lead us to him.

Theology of the Body: On Wednesdays from 1979 to 1984, St. John Paul II gave talks about how the human body reveals that human persons are created male and female in the image of God, with freedom for loving relationships and called to make a gift of ourselves on our way to happiness in heaven. These teachings are known as the Theology of the Body.

use: This is the opposite of love because it treats a person like an object for some pleasure or gain instead of respecting his or her dignity.

vice: A strong habit of doing what is not good. Vices enslave us to sin and rob us of the power to love. Even small vices lead to other vices.

virtue: A strong habit of doing what is good. Virtue empowers us to love God and others freely. Virtues are expressed by how we live in our visible bodies.

vocation: A calling from God to a particular path in life that will best fulfill your strengths, heal your weaknesses, and help you become a saint. Each person has a universal call to holiness that is received at Baptism. Vocations within the Church include marriage, consecrated life, and Holy Orders.

Notes

Lesson One

4   "It is Jesus ... you seek": John Paul II, World Youth Day Address (August 19, 2000), 5, vatican.va.

Lesson Two

18   "We come from God ...": John Paul II, Address to the Young People of New Orleans (September 12, 1987), 3, vatican.va.

Lesson Three

32   "The body, ... and only the body ...": John Paul II, General Audience (February 20, 1980), in *Man and Woman He Created Them: A Theology of the Body*, trans. Michael Waldstein (Boston: Pauline and Media, 2006), 19.4, p. 203.

Lesson Four

46   "It is Jesus who stirs in you ...": John Paul II, World Youth Day Address (August 19, 2000), 5.

Lesson Five

62   "Only the chaste man ...": Karol Wojtyla (Pope John Paul II), *Love and Responsibility*, trans. H.T. Willetts (San Francisco: Ignatius, 1993), 171.

Lesson Six

80   "A person's rightful due ...": Wojtyla, *Love and Responsibility*, 42.

Lesson Seven

98   "In the hidden recesses ...": John Paul II, Homily (February 10, 1986), vatican.va.

102   "Holiness is not the luxury of the few ...": Teresa of Calcutta, "Jesus Wants to Love with Our Hearts and Serve with Our Hands," *Tertium Millennium* 4 (September 1997), vatican.va.

103   "If we are what we ought to be ...": This is a popular paraphrase of "If you are what you ought to be, you will set fire to all Italy, and not only yonder." Catherine of Siena to Stefano Maconi, in *Saint Catherine of Siena as Seen in Her Letters*, trans. Vida D. Scudder (London: Dent, 1905), 305, Internet Archive.

108   "Ignorance of the Scriptures ...": Jerome, *Commentary on Isaiah*, trans. Thomas P. Scheck (Mahwah, NJ: Newman Press, 2015), prologue, biblia.com.

111   "The place God calls you to ...": Frederick Buechner, *Wishful Thinking: A Seeker's ABC* (San Francisco: Harper/SanFrancisco, 1993), 119.

Lesson Eight

114   "I ask you to have the courage …": John Paul II, World Youth Day Address (August 14, 1993),
       4, vatican.va.

116   "Dear young people …": John Paul II, World Youth Day Address (August 19, 2000), 5.

121   "Sometimes it is harder for us to smile …": Quoted in José Luis González-Balado, *Mother Teresa:
       In My Own Words* (Liguori, MO: Liguori, 1997), 75.

124   "Be not afraid!": John Paul II, Homily (October 22, 1978), vatican.va.

       "My dear young people …": John Paul II, World Youth Day Message (April 13, 2003), 6,
       vatican.va.

125   "No one apart from Christ … ": John Paul II, World Youth Day Message (April 13, 2003),
       6, vatican.va.

129   "In the face of modern developments …": Second Vatican Council, *Gaudium et Spes* 10, in
       Vatican II: The Basic Sixteen Documents, ed. Austin Flannery (Northport, NY: Costello, 2007), 172.

       "Failure to ask …": John Paul II, World Youth Day Address (August 14, 1993), First Part, 3,
       ewtn.com.

About the Authors and Presenters

AUTHORS

Brian Butler is the lead author and presenter of Ascension's *YOU: Life, Love, and the Theology of the Body* as well as a presenter in the *Chosen* Confirmation program. He graduated from the University of New Orleans and has a master's degree in theology from Notre Dame Seminary School of Theology along with many years' experience in teaching, youth ministry, and campus ministry. He is the executive director of Echo Community, a nonprofit organization dedicated to chastity and vocation formation for teens and young adults.

Jason Evert has traveled to six continents to bring the message of purity to millions of people for more than 25 years, including at World Youth Days in Australia, Spain, Poland, Panama, and Portugal. He has lectured at dozens of universities including Harvard, Princeton, and the U.S. Naval and Air Force Academies. He is a best-selling author of 20 books, including *Saint John Paul the Great*, *The Dating Blueprint*, and *Male, Female, Other?*. He is a frequent guest on radio programs, and his television appearances include MSNBC, Fox News, the BBC, and EWTN. Jason runs Chastity Project (Chastity.com), hosts the podcast "Lust is Boring," and leads an international alliance of young people who promote purity in more than forty countries.

Colin and Aimee MacIver teach theology at St. Scholastica Academy in Covington, Louisiana, where they serve as campus minister and service director, respectively. Their decades of combined experience include youth ministry, Confirmation preparation, speaking, training, visual art, and music ministry. They have authored many popular Ascension offerings over the years, including most recently *Connected: Catholic Social Teaching for This Generation* and *Receiving Jesus: My Guide to the Mass*.

Chika Anyanwu is a Catholic evangelist, former youth and young adult minister, and the author of *My Encounter: How I Met Jesus in Prayer*. She speaks internationally about the love and mercy of Jesus Christ and about prayer, Scripture, human dignity, and the difficult realities of faith and life. She has contributed to several Ascension programs, including *Connected: Catholic Social Teaching for This Generation* and *Venture: The Bible Timeline for High School*.

Tanner Kalina is the cofounder of the Saints Alive podcast, an alumnus of FOCUS (Fellowship of Catholic University Students), and a member of the National Eucharistic Congress team. He is a presenter on Ascension's *Encounter: The Bible Timeline for Middle School* series and has appeared in videos on Ascension Presents. He has also contributed to video projects for FOCUS, EWTN, CatholicMatch, and YDisciple.

Sr. Mary Grace Langrell, SV, grew up in Sydney, Australia, and graduated from the University of Notre Dame Australia. She worked in campus ministry before entering the Sisters of Life in 2013. Sr. Mary Grace then served vulnerable pregnant women in Toronto and now works for her community's evangelization mission, fostering a culture of life worldwide through mission trips, media, and online outreach. She also cohosts the Sisters of Life podcast, *Let Love*.

Mari Pablo grew up in southern Florida. She graduated from Franciscan University and holds a master's degree in theology from the Augustine Institute. She has contributed to several Ascension video series, including *Chosen: Your Journey to Confirmation, Connected: Catholic Social Teaching for This Generation*, and *Venture: The Bible Timeline for High School*, and to Ascension Presents. Mari has worked in youth ministry for more than fifteen years and currently serves parishes and universities with the Evangelical Catholic.

Envision Program Credits

EXECUTIVE PRODUCER AND PUBLISHER
Jonathan Strate

GENERAL MANAGERS
Jeffrey Cole
Dcn. John Harden

PROJECT MANAGER
Veronica Salazar

SENIOR PRODUCT MANAGER
Patrick McCabe

PRODUCT MANAGER
Lauren Welsh

Envision Video Series
SENIOR VIDEO PRODUCER
Matthew Pirrall

VIDEO CREATIVE DIRECTOR
Matthew Longua

PRODUCTION COMPANY
Coronation Media

FEATURED PRESENTERS
Chika Anyanwu
Brian Butler
Jason Evert
Tanner Kalina
Sr. Mary Grace Langrell, SV
Aimee MacIver
Colin MacIver
Mari Pablo

THEOLOGICAL CONSULTANTS
Jeffrey Cole
Dcn. John Harden
Carlos Taja

Envision Print Components
AUTHORS AND WRITERS
Brian Butler
Jason Evert
Aimee MacIver
Colin MacIver

CONTENT REVIEW
Jeffrey Cole
Dcn. John Harden
Carlos Taja
Elisa Tremblay

GRAPHIC DESIGN
Sarah Stueve
Stella Ziegler

EDITORIAL
Christina Eberle
Rebecca Robinson

MARKETING
Mark Leopold
Julia Morgensai